Shari'a Law and the Modern Nation-State:
A Malaysian Symposium

Shari'a Law and the Modern Nation-State
A Malaysian Symposium

Edited by
Norani Othman

A book based on
the papers and discussion
at *Sisters In Islam* First Symposium:
Symposium on
The Modern Nation State
and Islam

Sisters In Islam
SIS Forum (Malaysia) Berhad
Kuala Lumpur
1994

Published with the support of the
FRIEDRICH-NAUMANN-STIFTUNG
(Germany)

First published by SIS Forum (Malaysia) Berhad
172 Lorong Maarof
Bangsar Park
59000 Kuala Lumpur
This book is based on the papers and discussion at
Sisters In Islam First Symposium
Symposium on The Modern Nation State and Islam
Editor: Norani Othman
Published with the support of the
Friedrich-Naumann-Stiftung (Germany)

Perpustakaan Negara Malaysia/National Library of Malaysia
Data Pengkatalogan dalam Penerbitan/Cataloging-in-Publication Data
Norani Othman [editor], 1950–
Islam and the Modern Nation State: A Malaysian Symposium
ISBN: 967-947-187-X
1. Islamic Law and the Modern State.
2. Islam and Politics.
3. Islamic law in Malaysia.

Typesetting and layout by Kim Unique Graphic Services
Cover design by Hoh Yin Peng
Printed by Setiakawan Printers Sdn. Bhd.

PRICE: RM 20.00

Whoever does not understand the *shari'a* historically does not understand the *shari'a*; whoever does not understand Islam historically does not really understand Islam.

— Malek Bennabi

Contents

Epilogue: Shari'a Law in the Modern World

Preface

Since the *hijra* Muslims have been concerned with the social and political organisation of their societies. The first Islamic community, under the close and careful guidance of the Prophet Muhammad, was a politically dynamic one, incorporating effective structures for the interaction of Muslims and non-Muslims, and between *muhajirun* (the later Muslim emigrants to Medina) and the *ansar* ("helpers", or close associates of the Prophet already resident there).

As the architect of the Medinan Charter, the Prophet drew upon the various ethical codes and the social framework of his time. This Charter, later to be known as the "Constitution of Medina", was open and flexible. It provided for the democratic existence and peaceful co-existence of different ethnic and religious communities. Over time it became for Muslims a beacon—a reference point for deriving methods of governance.

The state founded by the Prophet was essentially a city-state and, as such, it had to work within the limitations imposed by its initially restricted size and scope. Nevertheless, it did provide the basic structure on which the Prophet's immediate successors—the first four rightly-guided caliphs—built the Islamic empire, eventually embracing within its fold diverse lands and heterogenous peoples.

The organisation of many Muslim nations over the last fifty years since the end of colonialism has been based, however, on the "Western" state model. The postcolonial development of most Muslim countries saw increasing tension between this adopted political order and the renewed efforts of many of their citizens to define and strengthen their Islamic identity.

In their attempt to find an alternative to that derivatively Western political framework, many Muslims have looked for guidance towards the Medinan model. Yet the vast historical and social changes which span the time between the establishment of the first Islamic community and the contemporary world order require a creative and historically sensitive interpretation of that model.

How should an Islamic state be run? How can we today, as modern people committed to both our religious heritage and to a vision of progress for its inheritors, interpret the essentials of the Medinan model? How are we now to understand and realise the Qur'anic ideals of equality, justice and political sovereignty of the *umma*?

These questions have been the focus of serious and searching concern to *Sisters In Islam*, as they are to many contemporary Muslims. It was a recognition of the urgent need to address those questions which prompted *Sisters In Islam* to organise a symposium on "The Modern Nation State and Islam" in Kuala Lumpur in October 1992. The occasion proved an exciting one, both challenging and productive, and the book which we now offer here to a wider readership than the symposium participants is not simply a record of its proceedings. It is also evidence of the continuing relevance to contemporary Malaysia of the issues that were debated at our symposium.

As symposium organisers, we were convinced that it is the religious and social duty of today's and tomorrow's Muslims not simply to receive, in a passive and unenquiring manner, the religious heritage which comes to us from the life and revelations of the Prophet Muhammad but to engage actively with it, in an effort to understand and deepen its contemporary relevance. Looking back upon it, we remain convinced that our symposium was one of the more rewarding Malaysian endeavours of recent times to probe the hidden treasures of our faith. In particular, we were encouraged that, consistent with our hopes expressed at the outset, the discussion generated by the various symposium presentations addressed these issues in the noble spirit of enquiry and learning that is enjoined by Islam.

That symposium would not have been possible without the help and support of many people—friends, colleagues, family and relatives. We warmly record our gratitude to the following persons and institutions who have encouraged us and contributed in many ways to our various projects, and especially this one. To all of them goes our profound appreciation of their support.

Our sincere and special thanks go to to Dr. Abdullahi Ahmed An-Nai'm, for working with us to realise this project, and to all the paper-writers, panelists, moderators, rapporteurs, various volunteers and other individuals who tirelessly provided us with much organisational and clerical support. To name them all here would be impossible, but to all of them go our heart-felt thanks: we shall always remember and cherish your unwavering support and encouragement.

We also thank those individuals who remain anonymous here at their own personal request. We value your various financial contributions which helped greatly towards covering the costs of this symposium, as well as the moral support which your tangible donations conveyed. Again, we can only say: *ribuan terima kasih*.

We also record our gratitude to the following individuals and institutions for their help, support and contributions:

Anuar Fazal, UNDP: United Nations Development Project

Datuk Anuar Othman

Assoc. Prof. Hairi Abdullah, Head, Department of Anthropology & Sociology, UKM: Universiti Kebangsaan Malaysia

Prof. Ishak Shari, President, Persatuan Sains Sosial Malaysia (Malaysian Social Science Association)

Joseph Selvadurai, NPC Hotel

Assoc. Prof. Kamaruddin M. Said, General Secretary, PSSM

Khalid Ahmad, Managing Director, New Straits Times Sdn. Bhd.

Razak Halipah, PSSM

Dr. Robert Haas, Friedrich-Naumann-Stiftung, Kuala Lumpur

The staff of ISIS: Institute of Strategic and International Studies, Kuala Lumpur

The staff of the Department of Anthropology & Sociology, UKM

Datuk Haji Abdul Malik Ahmad
Ahmad Shazilly Ismail Bakti
Aishah Ali
Alina Ranee
Asnah Ahmad
Hajjah Ainon Kuntom
Datin Dulcie Abraham
Hassan Ibrahim
Hajjah Ilani Isahak
Khadijah Mohd. Salleh
Nimalka Fernando
Datuk Nordin Omar
Rahmah Hussein
Datin Rozana Haji Khalid
Syed Jabar Shahabudin
Zainah Anwar
Zarinah Anwar

One final but most significant debt remains to be acknowledged. We thank the Friedrich-Naumann-Stiftung for its generous funding towards the publication of this book, as well as its contribution for the holding of our symposium in October 1992. To the Stiftung and to its Kuala Lumpur representative, Dr. Robert Haas, special thanks are due, and are here gratefully extended.

In all their various activities, *Sisters In Islam* prefer to work cooperatively, as a group of diverse but consensual individuals. Consistent with that approach, this book has been collectively edited by Askiah Adam, Norani Othman, Rose Ismail, Salbiah Ahmad and Sharifah Zuriah Aljeffri, all members of *Sisters In Islam* who organised and sponsored the symposium on which it is based. By the group's decision, Norani Othman has assumed special responsibilities for the preparation of this volume from the unedited conference proceedings. In this connection the editor also thanks Professor Clive Kessler and Rustam A. Sani for their assistance in preparing the manuscript for publication.

Sisters In Islam publish this book in the hope, and confidence, that the arguments presented and the issues raised in it will receive serious consideration: in particular, from a readership of thinking Muslims who in equal measure value their religious heritage and recognise the need to shape intelligently a sustainable future for its inheritors. In Malaysia as elsewhere, we believe, the shaping of that future is not something to be left solely to those conventionally recognised as "religiously learned", or to any special section of the *umma*. Rather, the development—consistent with Qur'anic understandings of social responsibility and action—of a modern tradition of active, participatory citizenship transcending all sectional divisions within the worldwide *umma* seems to us to be indispensable if contemporary Muslims are to find ways of effectively addressing the challenges of today and tomorrow.

Our reading about and contacts with developments in other Muslim countries convince us that our diagnosis and prescription are both appropriate and necessary elsewhere in the *umma*; but certainly, the main focus of our concern is Malaysia itself. As pressures mount in our own country for the anachronistic implementation, as the twentieth century closes, of forms and understandings of Islamic law (including the *hudud* punishments of mutilation by amputation, stoning and crucifixion) that date back to the early centuries of Islamic civilisation, the need to foster an enlightened and contemporary understanding of enduring Qur'anic imperatives seems both necessary and urgent.

This book and the response that it evokes in the minds of its readers will, we hope, prove a significant contribution to the emergence of such an approach: one that is both authentically grounded in the Qur'anic worldview and at the same time based upon a discerning appreciation of the challenges of ever advancing modernity, upon which today's Muslims cannot, and should not, turn their backs.

Norani Othman
for *Sisters In Islam*

Kuala Lumpur
February 1994

A Note on Transliteration of Arabic Terms

Of the many technical decisions which the chief editor had to take, perhaps the most difficult was that involving the transliteration of a number of terms concerned with the main theme of the symposium: those dealing with Islamic law and the Muslim religion. In short, a reasonably simple and consistent, even if somewhat arbitrary, rule-of-thumb had to be adopted. The choice made in this case was as follows. Even though this book is, as its subtitle proclaims, a Malaysian symposium, we hope that, like the implications of its subject, the readership that it will reach will extend well beyond the boundaries of Malaysia itself. Accordingly, rather than the standard Malaysian forms for those terms, we have instead adopted forms or conventional spellings deriving from the simplified transliterations for terms of Arabic provenance that are widely recognised throughout the worldwide English-speaking community of Muslims and students of Islam. In so doing, we at the same time sought to minimise the use of complex diacritical marks that characterise the more specialist conventions for rendering classical Arabic in Roman characters. Hence, for example, the opting here for *shari'a*, not *syariah*, and *shura*, not *syura*. The system adopted here will not please everyone, not even the authors themselves whose contributions to this collection are subjected to it; but at least, it is hoped, the benefits and virtues of adhering consistently to the one set of usages throughout this book will be appreciated.

Notes on Contributors

ABDULLAHI AHMED AN-NA'IM was born in the Sudan, received his doctorate in law from the University of Edinburgh, and taught law for nine years (1976–1985) at the University of Khartoum. Since leaving the Sudan he has been a visiting fellow at Columbia University, New York, at the University of Saskatchewan, Canada, the University of California at Los Angeles (UCLA), the University of Uppsala, Sweden, and Harvard University and has served as Ford Foundation representative in Cairo, Egypt. He now holds a senior position with the international human rights group Africa Watch in Washington D.C. He is the author of a number of books including *Toward an Islamic Reformation: Civil Liberties, Human Rights, and International Law* (Syracuse U.P., Syracuse NY, 1990) and is also translator of Mahmoud Mohamed Taha's *The Second Message of Islam* (Syracuse U.P., Syracuse NY, 1987).

AMINA WADUD-MUHSIN now teaches Islamic and religious studies at Virginia Commonwealth University in Virginia, U.S.A. She received her doctorate from the University of Michigan, taught for three years at the International Islamic University in Kuala Lumpur, and is the author of *Qur'an and Woman* (Fajar Bakti, Kuala Lumpur, 1992).

ASKIAH ADAM was born in Malacca, received her early education in Malaysia and completed her secondary education in England, where she also attended university, earning her B.A. and M.A. degrees in politics and philosophy. She is now completing a doctoral thesis on "Women and Islam" at the University of Canterbury, Kent. She works as a senior analyst at ISIS: Institute of Strategic and International Studies in Kuala Lumpur.

ASMA LARIF-BÉATRIX was born and received her early education in Tunisia. She earned a higher doctorate (*doctorat d' état*) in political science from the Sorbonne, Paris for her thesis on "State Formation and its Cultural Context: The Elite Political and Administrative Personnel of Contemporary Tunisia". She has been living in Kuala Lumpur for the last four years, and is writing a book comparing patterns of premodern and early modern state formation in Europe and Southeast Asia—a study which she intends will eventually explore contrasting patterns of contemporary state organisation.

CHANDRA MUZAFFAR is a well-known social analyst and commentator who now serves as head of Just World Trust. He received his doctorate from the University of Singapore, has returned after some years' interruption to teaching at Universiti Sains Malaysia in Penang, was the founder and leader throughout its early years of the social reform group *Aliran*, and is the author of a number of significant works including *Protector? An Analysis of the Concept and Practice of Loyalty in Leader-Led Relationships within Malay Society* (Aliran, Penang, 1980) and *Islamic Resurgence in Malaysia* (Fajar Bakti, Kuala Lumpur, 1987).

K. HARIDAS holds an honours degree in law from the University of London, the certificate of legal practice, and a postgraduate diploma in Syariah Law from the International Islamic University in Kuala Lumpur. He is a member of the Communications Advertising and Marketing Foundation in the U.K. (M.C.A.M.), a fellow of the Institute of Public Relations Malaysia (F.I.P.R.), and a member of the Malaysian Institute of Management (M.M.I.M.).

MOHAMMAD HASHIM KAMALI was born in Afghanistan and completed his LL.M. and doctorate in law and Middle Eastern studies at the University of London. He has taught at McGill University in Montreal, Canada and is now Professor of Law at the

International Islamic University, Kuala Lumpur. He is the author of a number of scholarly books including *Law in Afghanistan: A Study of the Constitutions, Matrimonial Law and the Judiciary* (Brill, Leiden, 1985) and *Principles of Islamic Jurisprudence* (Pelanduk Publications, Petaling Jaya, 1989) as well as numerous internationally published articles in the same field.

MUHAMMAD SYUKRI SALLEH teaches social science at Universiti Sains Malaysia in Penang. The doctoral thesis that he completed at Oxford on the economic philosophy and development strategy of the *Darul Arqam* has been published as *An Islamic Approach to Rural Development: The Arqam Way* (ASOIB International, London, 1992).

NORANI OTHMAN is a graduate of the University of Malaya, earned her M. Phil. at the University of Hull, and later also pursued postgraduate studies for some years at the University of Oxford. She is a lecturer at the Department of Sociology and Anthropology at Universiti Kebangsaan Malaysia (UKM). In addition to her more popular commentaries upon current issues including women's political participation and on the politics of Islamisation, she has also published academic articles on women and working life, on the development and limitations of the Malaysian social science tradition, and on women, gender and society. In recent years she has been active in organising academic seminars and conferences in these areas for the Malaysian Social Science Association, of whose executive she is a member.

ROSE ISMAIL is a B.A. (Honours) graduate of the University of Melbourne and received her Masters in Journalism degree from Boston University in 1982. She has worked for a number of years as a senior journalist with the *New Straits Times* in Kuala Lumpur. She recently spent a year as a fellow at the University of Michigan, where she both read and also wrote extensively about contemporary intellectual movements and sociopolitical developments within the Islamic world.

SALBIAH AHMAD was born in Singapore and received her LL.B. degree from the University of Singapore, and was admitted as an advocate and solicitor of the Supreme Court of the Republic of Singapore. She later earned her Master of Comparative Law degree in the field of civil law as well as a Diploma in Syariah and the Administration of Muslim Law from the International Islamic University in Kuala Lumpur, where she also taught law for seven years. She now works as a program associate with APWLD: The Asia Pacific Forum on Women, Law and Development in Kuala Lumpur.

SHARIFAH ZURIAH ALJEFFRI, following some early legal studies in London and after earning a Diploma in Public Relations, worked for many years as a cultural affairs advisor to USIS: the United States Information Service in Kuala Lumpur. She is a well-known Malaysian artist who has exhibited both in her own country and overseas, and is deeply involved in a variety of Malaysian cultural organisations and activities. In 1992 and 1993 she offered exhibitions of her work in Malaysia and also in Vienna to raise funds for the Bosnian Relief Fund to alleviate the suffering of victims of atrocity. She is also active in a number of areas of social responsibility, including service as an advisor to the magistrates of the juvenile court. In 1993 she was awarded a Fulbright grant enabling her to undertake a lecture tour to the U.S.A. where she spoke at a number of universities about the Bosnian tragedy, women and Islam, and Malaysian society and culture generally.

1

Introduction: Eternal Qur'anic Principles Today

*Sisters In Islam**

The role of Islam in the nation-state is a very important issue, particularly now that the world political order has been left on one leg with the collapse of communism. This has created a vacuum which, some Muslim scholars say, can be filled by Islamic ideology.

Most Muslims would readily support this, because we believe Islam provides a counter-balance to capitalism and liberal democracy. But many of us are also aware of the failure on the part of Muslims to present Islam as a viable and credible alternative.

Muslims have quibbled among themselves over trivial matters, strained their relationships over problems that can be readily resolved and have even gone to war over tiny parcels of land.

While some blame can be apportioned to the media for stereotyping and simplifying issues, Muslims themselves must also take responsibility for the negative image Islam evokes among many people. Constant rancour, distrust and disunity among us have blinded the world to seeing and understanding the balanced social, economic and political worldview that exists in Islam.

---

* This introductory statement of the aims of the symposium was prepared by *Sisters In Islam* and presented at the opening session on the group's behalf by Sharifah Zuriah Aljeffri.

In fact, what some Muslims have succeeded in doing is to alarm others with the many laws and policies that have been introduced in some Muslim countries that are supposed to be "Islamic". Yet, there is growing evidence to suggest that these laws and policies may not have been thought through carefully and are detrimental to certain groups or sections of the community.

Above all, there is considerable fear that Islam allows for an unequal relationship between Muslims and non-Muslims and between men and women. Because of this, the idea of an Islamic state frightens many people because they see it as regressive, restrictive and rigid.

But is this so?

The role of Islam in the nation-state is particularly important to Malaysia. We have seen the rise of a new Islamic consciousness for over a decade now. We have also seen volumes of literature on the subject. But beyond the words, what is the reality?

Can we implement Islamic policies and laws to cover both Muslims and non-Muslims without making non-Muslims feel threatened?

Take the Malaysian state of Kelantan, for example, where since the return to power of the Islamic Party (PAS) in 1990 proposals for the legislative enforcement of the traditional *hudud* punishments have been voiced. It is a microcosm of this dilemma. While many of us would support the sincere endeavour of the state government to introduce Islamic law to cover all facets of life, we worry about the practicability of its implementation.

We are not questioning God's laws and his guidance but we are concerned with those aspects of the *shari'a* developed by the early Muslim jurists which may no longer be relevant to the problems of today or capable of resolving them.

The basis of Islamic social and political thought owes much to classical jurists. Their interpretations of Qur'anic ethical and legal imperatives formed the bulk of what came to be known in the early centuries of Islamic civilisation as *shari'a;* but those interpretations were made in the context of the world at that time, and much has changed since then.

However, any analysis or questioning of the *shari'a* is viewed by many as sacrilegious. Yet it is our contention that any body of thought put together by human beings cannot remain inviolate in the face of a changing world.

For the religion to grow, as it must grow, and for Muslims to grow, as we must grow, there is a critical need to ask important questions. How should an Islamic state be run? How can we interpret the essentials of the Medinan model in the context of Qur'anic ideas of equality, justice and political sovereignty of the citizens?

The richness of the Qur'anic message is endless. We have yet to discover the full meaning of God's words. Just as there have been numerous efforts in the past to study the religion and there will continue to be more in the future, we hope this symposium will be seen as one of many endeavours to seek the hidden treasures of the faith.

We also hope that discussions generated by the various essays presented here will address issues in the spirit of enquiry and learning as enjoined by the *Qur'an.*

The views expressed in the various essays presented here are those of their respective authors, and not necessarily those of *Sisters In Islam* or any of its members. We are happy to provide an opportunity for the expression of these diverse and always challenging viewpoints. Recognition of the diversity encompassed within the *umma* and of the pluralism of the Islamic intellectual tradition has been basic to the outlook of *Sisters In Islam*.

Part I:

Islam in History and Society

2

Towards an Islamic Reformation: Islamic Law in History and Society Today

*Abdullahi Ahmed An-Na'im**

The subject of my address that was suggested by the organisers of this symposium is taken from the title of my recent book, *Toward an Islamic Reformation* (1990). However, this title needs to be explained. The term "reformation" evokes certain associations with Christian Europe during its period of reformation and secularisation. The equivalent in Arabic is *islah*. This Arabic term requires some clarification.

Religious renewal and legal reform

The term "reformation" evokes images of Europe in the period of 17th to 18th century: of a civil society where the authority of the church was challenged and a separation between church and state was being instituted. This is not what we should understand by *islah*. For some contemporary religious and political activists, *islah*

* Dr. Abdullahi An-Na'im's review of the socially and historically conditioned character of the *shari'a*, and of the need for and also legitimacy of pursuing the reform of Islamic law consistent with the requirements of modern life (but on the basis of the enduring Qur'anic foundations of the Muslim faith), was presented as the keynote address of the symposium as a whole. It also opened the symposium's first part on "Islamic Law in History and Society".

evokes images not of secularisation or of the declining public role of religion but of revivalism: of the desire, even attempt, to revert to an assumed and allegedly pure Islamic state or community. This attempt among many contemporary Muslims to return to what they understand as their religious origins rests upon a fervent wish: "if only we could go back to our secure and glorious past," they in effect say, "we might achieve all that we want to do; we could attain independence, political stability and cultural autonomy".

Neither of these notions—either of a retreat from religion, as in the Western sense, or a retreat into a more reassuring but idealised past, as with many who are identified with today's movement for Islamic resurgence—is adequate for our needs. We do not want to go back, nor can we. Nor do we want a repetition or to engage in any mimicking of the European Christian experience. Rather, we need and must have our own indigenous and authentic approach. It is something that we can actually have, provided that we are capable of meeting in the spirit and best traditions of our faith the intellectual challenge that it poses to us.

The subject is vast. I will therefore try to identify only the key issues and give my own position in relation to them. But I would like also to make it clear that the emphasis throughout this presentation is upon methodological and not the substantive questions. In such a methodological approach it is not so much what I say or what anyone says but the way things are said and articulated and how discussions are held that is crucial.

Islamic law and society

Why the reference to Islamic law in the title of my book and this keynote address? The assumption here is that Islamic law is relevant to what we must do and what we are engaged in. As a lawyer, I happen to believe that law is important and central in relation to the process of change. But I must also clarify what I mean by Islamic law and its relationship or function in society.

Islamic law is not law in the technical sense. The relationship between Islamic law and society is, has always been and will remain both difficult and complex. It is not a straighforward, causal relationship enabling us confidently to assert that if we establish Islamic law, then any particular desired outcome will therefore necessarily follow. Establishing Islamic law is not something a state or government or legal system can do because of the very nature of the law itself.

As a living institution, Islamic law encompasses every aspect of people's lives—faith, rituals, ethics as well as the so-called strictly legal subject matter. Because of its multifaceted nature, a state cannot simply establish or enforce it. The relationship between Islamic law and society or societies (and I emphasise the plural) is important. Throughout the world we find different societies which have been and now are Muslim in varying degrees and in different ways. They have all found their own ways of giving expression to our common faith. The fact that all Muslims are not Muslims in the exact same way is, I think, a healthy and positive aspect of Islam—because it indicates the ability of Islam to adapt to and respond to people's needs, aspirations and peculiarities. Yet, transcending such variations these different societies also display certain commonalities, for there are certain universalities to being a Muslim. There are ways in which Islam and Islamic law have universal significance to all Islamic societies.

The relationship between Islamic law and society has historically been problematic and will always be so. We cannot expect it to be otherwise. Sometimes to our surprise, we find in the recent phenomenon that is known as the Islamic resurgence various anachronistic projections of modern ideas and notions into Islamic history, just as we encounter a desire to enforce archaic or anachronistic instutions from early Islamic civilisation within the modern world. One example of the anachronistic reading back of the present into the Islamic past is the assertion or assumption that democracy and human rights have always existed in Islam, based upon the claim that Islam preceded all other civilisations in these respects.

Conceptually this cannot be valid, and historically it is incorrect. Islam is capable of adopting and promoting these concepts now and in the future. Indeed, the ethos or worldview or ethical outlook of the *Qur'an* is particularly well-suited for the articulation of these ideals: for their expression and championing in Islamic terms to modern, religiously plural civilisation. But it is not true that these concepts were a Muslim creation or were always part of the historical experience of Muslims. So let us be honest. When we study our histories and societies—their achievements and failures, their problems and successes—we should not indulge in wishful thinking or have illusions about a golden age in which everything was fine and all Muslims were honest and diligent, fair and just. We know from our histories that things were not so.

We must also be clear about the role of Islamic law in relation to Islamic societies which were not exclusively Muslim. Muslims did not in the past, and do not now, act or behave as Muslims all the time. It is true that Islam is a central fact of Muslim lives, but it is not the sole determining factor. As human beings, people are concerned with their well-being, their physical security and their welfare; and these may not be served by their faith as they see or practise it.

As evidence of this we may simply recall the unedifying aspects of what is known in history as *al-fitnah al-kubra* (the grand or great upheaval). Within decades of the Prophet's death, Muslims were struggling with one another for political and economic power. The *sahaba* (companions of the Prophet—even the most outstanding of them—went to battle on opposite sides. Moreover, three of the four caliphs who succeded the Prophet (known as the *khulafa rashidun* or "rightly-guided caliphs"—and who were among the Prophet's earliest companions and the early Muslim community's more capable leaders—were assassinated. The very elementary idea of a peaceful transfer of power was not practised by the "best of communities" (as the community of Medina is known), the best that we have had in our history. Within thirty years of the Prophet's death, absolute monarchies emerged and consolidated themselves, first the Umayyad and following it the Abbasid, which together ruled most of the Muslim world for more than five centuries.

My point here is that issues are not that simple; they have never been that simple. We should not, therefore, delude ourselves into thinking that all we need to do is to re-enact early Islamic history. What we need to do is to engage in a very protracted and careful process aimed at the rediscovery and reformation of the principles of Islamic law, in an endeavour to find appropriate and constructive ways of implementing them under modern conditions. Islamic law must be rethought, in the first instance by rediscovering and reanimating its enduring principles, if it is ever in any way to be reactualised. We have to realise immediately the urgency of the matter.

Madhab and sunna

When we talk about Islamic law or *shari'a*, we must realise that we are talking of a human phenomenon. Many of those who engage in contemporary Islamic discourse claim to present or try to portray *shari'a* as divine law. It is true that the sources of the *shari'a* are divine to some extent, but not exclusively. The *Qur'an* and authentic *sunna* are divine in our belief. But the other sources of *shari'a* such as *qiyas* (analogy) and *ijma* (consensus) are self-evidently human. Moreover, the methodology, the concept, the principles, and the techniques of the *shari'a* are also human since they were developed by jurists. *Shari'a* is the product of human reasoning upon a foundation of divine inspiration.

The *shari'a* is said to be based on the *Qur'an* and on the *sunna* of the Prophet. Now, the *Qur'an*, we know, was recorded in the sense of being committed in a definitive written form a few decades after the Prophet's death (during the reign of Othman ibn Affan), and that text is universally taken by Muslims as the legitimate and authentic text of the *Qur'an*. Although Muslims of good faith may differ over issues of *qiraat* (styles of recitation), the substance of the *Qur'an* is taken as authentic.

But what people understand by the *shari'a* when they urge its absolute acceptance as divine law is not just the authoritative Qur'anic text, either by itself or even amplified by reference to what can be accepted as the authentic *sunna* of the Prophet. Such people have in mind certain codifications of law that are based upon—and said to amplify—their foundation in *Qur'an* and *sunna* that were offered by the great founding jurists of Islam. But we need to be careful on this point. Just to think chronologically, the four surviving schools of Islamic jurisprudence (*madhab*) to which all Sunni Muslims belong today—the Maliki, Hanbali, Hanafi and Shafe'i—were established by jurists who did their work of codification towards the end of the second century and during the first half of the third century of Islam. That is, their systematisations of the law were codified about 150 to 250 years after the Prophet's death.

These jurists did their work and articulated their views regarding the meaning of the *Qur'an* and the *sunna* at a time when the *sunna* itself was not yet systematically collected or its authenticity verified. The *a'immah* of *hadith*—that is, the jurists who collected and verified the *sunna*—collected their compilations only after the death of the founding jurists of the four major schools. Even the term *sunna* itself and its meaning (that is, whether it refers to the *sunna* of the community of Medina, or the *sunna* relating only to the Prophet himself exclusively) was an issue whose ambiguity was clarified only later, by Shafe'i who was the third of the four founding jurists.

The science of systematic compilation of the *sunna* (known as *khutubah sahihah* of *sunna*) began only after the four founding jurists had completed their work. Yet there are those who, quite unhistorically, now urge the absolute acceptance as divine law of understandings of *shari'a* which are based upon reasoning from this only slowly established foundation of *sunna*. That is, contrary to unambiguous historical facts, they contend that the great jurists produced their codifications of *shari'a* on the basis of an entirely fixed and categorical body of law or jurisprudence supposedly provided by the *sunna*. That claim, as an historical perspective shows, is patently false. But it remains the necessary foundation for any assertion that all of what has come to be known as *shari'a*, being divine and mandatory, must therefore as a matter of religious faith and obligation be implemented in our own times. But if that claim is seen historically for what it is and is accordingly rejected, the argument that, in some conventional form or other, the *shari'a* must now be applied simply collapses. All projects aiming at the modern implementation and enforcement of such formulations of *shari'a*, whatever understanding or misunderstandings their proponents may have of their own motivations, are therefore simply human projects lacking all divine sanction.

In their own works, the founding jurists made it clear that they had no intention whatsoever of establishing even schools of thought or traditions of legal interpretation. Even less did they have any view of their work as establishing a *shari'a*. They neither claimed to be doing so themselves, nor did they expect that the fruits of their work of developing a jurisprudence would even apply beyond their own immediate communities—still less that they would be made to apply forever and universally, as eternally binding expressions of divine intentions. They had no conception whatsoever that they were establishing eternal divine law. They were simply expressing their views of what they understood the *Qur'an* to mean in the very particular terms and specific context of their own time and place.

As legal scholars, they raised hypothetical issues and questions and attempted to offer practicable answers to them. But they had no political power and, in fact, shunned judicial office. But the opinions arising out of their scholastic analyses were subsequently taken by later thinkers who treated them as exclusive, divine and authoritative *shari'a*. In this fundamentally important sense, the *shari'a* is human, not divine. Accordingly, all ahistorical formulations of and attitudes towards *shari'a* can be contested, and should.

Shari'a

When we look at the actual history of Islamic societies, we need to raise the question of the extent to which Islamic law or the *shari'a* was consistently and comprehensively applied at any point of time. We will find that Islamic societies were not always consistent in their treatment of the *shari'a*. They never conformed to the *shari'a* in a comprehensive and total manner. We have to ask ourselves why. We must also look at efforts to reimplement the *shari'a* today in the light of the nature of historical *shari'a* and the previous experience of Islamic societies.

As we engage in the reformulation and reactualisation of Islamic law—in any endeavour towards its renewed implementation—the radically transformed circumstances of Islamic societies today must be acknowledged. We now live in a highly complex, global, interdependent world. No one can afford isolation, or even plausibly attempt it. We must take this radically transfomed reality into account when we consider what the *shari'a* means today and how it can be again implemented. The *shari'a* cannot be implemented in any "ready-made" or "off-the-shelf" form, but must first be rethought and reconceptualised. Any realisation or reinstitutionalisation of the *shari'a* will first require radical reform. This is imperative.

Competing imperatives for change confront us today. As Muslims, we wish to live by our faith and to relate to it constructively, yet we have to do so under radically transformed conditions. These are what I call "competing imperatives for change". On the one hand, we are concerned with Islamic authenticity and legitimacy. That is how we and our people, our constituency, think and feel. On the other hand, we must give effect to that concern for authenticity in a way which responds to our needs and aspirations in today's world. This is the fundamental issue which confronts Islamic reform and Islamic thought today.

Ijtihad

I now want to address the prospect of resolution of certain fundamental tensions in the historical formulations of *shari'a*. I say "historical formulations" because I do not believe them to be the exclusive or the sole formulations of Islamic law, although I believe them to have been valid and relevant in their own historical settings and context. This implies that there can be other versions of *shari'a*; versions that draw from the same sources and which legitimately use Islamic concepts and techniques but as they are understood and implemented by Muslims today. Earlier formulations of historical *shari'a* were not eternal and universal, but appropriate expressions—as the best and most contemporary Muslims minds of their time understood them—of the enduring Qur'anic imperatives to which *shari'a* as a system of law must at any time give form. Accordingly, if *shari'a* is to be made actual and implemented in the modern world, we are both entitled and obliged to rethink it: to find ways of expressing and embodying those imperatives which are appropriate to our own time and circumstances.

Muslims who are concerned with these issues (and unfortunately not all Muslims are) tend to say that all we need to do is to exercise *ijtihad*; that our problem is that the gate of *ijtihad* was closed around the 9th or 10th century C.E. and that if only we would open the gates of *ijtihad* we would be able to solve all our problems (the questions, for example, concerning of the rights of women and those of non-Muslims). But as I explained in my book, we have to be clear about what we mean by *ijtihad*. *Ijtihad* within the framework of the *shari'a* as it was established and understood by the founding jurists will not help us. It will not take us far enough because those jurists defined *ijtihad*, its sources and its techniques in their own setting: within their own frame of intellectual reference and in accordance with their own particular historical and contextually shaped sense of the meaning of the *Qur'an*.

Ijtihad must mean the phenomenon of keeping an open mind—of being original, being daring and imaginative in dealing with and relating to the text, in pursuing and understanding textual analysis. Conceptually, this process of deriving meaning through textual analysis inherently involves two components: the text and the reader or the interpreter. Like texts and the prior interpretations already encountered by us that influence our own readings of them, the reader is also the product of his or her context. If we remember this fact, we will appreciate that a sensitivity to historical context—ours and also its—is necessary for understanding what a text might possibly mean in any historical setting in which it might become implicated.

Here I am really concerned about the adequacy and the relevance of the various interpretive techniques that we are told will answer or resolve all our problems. We may have to begin thinking of *ijtihad* not in the traditional terms of classical Islamic jurisprudence but in terms more appropriate to our own times and situation. That is, we may need to reconceptualise it not as a technique, even a special right, exercised on an individual basis by members of a scholastic elite with some monopoly entitlement to recourse to the use of intellectual discretion. Instead—consistent with the ethos and tenour of our democratic times, as well as the participatory character of the founding *umma*—we may now have to understand it as a process of dialogic reasoning and cooperative deliberation within the *umma* generally.

In such a reconceptualised *ijtihad*, the *ulama* or jurisprudential scholars would not be sidelined or excluded (so they need not fear any such fate); rather, their role would be to exercise *ijtihad* in concert and through democratic engagement with the generality of believers in the *umma*. Whatever intellectual leadership that they, like other legal scholars and specialists, might give would be exercised from within and among the *umma*, not from any automatic or guaranteed position as sole repositories of truth and wisdom at the head of the community of Islam. In that way, they will make themselves accountable to, and within, the *umma* to those whom they wish to inform and instruct.

Whether the *ulama* will prove capable of democratising their practice and procedures in this way remains, however, to be seen. But whether such a reconceptualised understanding of *ijtihad* becomes operative will not depend solely or even largely upon them, but upon the intellectual openness and spiritual energy, as well as the example, of those Muslims who are concerned with rethinking their faith and its implications in contemporary terms.

In the part of the world where I come from (the Sudan and the Middle East) we often lack that intellectual openness when we debate our faith. What we lack in clarity and critical ability we seemingly compensate, however, in our intolerance of difference and our refusal of dialogue over disagreements. This is made worse by the inclination to exchange hasty charges of heresy or treason. Instead of addressing rival views and their presuppositions on their own terms, we often prefer to resort to abuse: to dismiss the message by discrediting the messenger. This way of avoiding the need to deal with religious views that challenge our own is a very negative aspect of our culture, one that Muslims everywhere must redress before we can begin to address anything else. We have to be open to critical, well-informed, rational views that are offered in good conscience about our traditions, their significance and implications.

Women and non-Muslims in an Islamic state

Some of the issues that I want to raise will be explored in the discussion. But let me give an illustration here. There are two major areas of tension and conflict between what an Islamic state seeks to implement, or the premise on which it rests, and what *shari'a* has to say on the subject: the question of rights of women and the rights of non-Muslims. A modern nation-state is necessarily pluralistic and diverse, and it has to deal with a very complex, interdependent world: with a world system of economic development and with the various political, strategic and security concerns that arise within it.

To envisage in this context an Islamic state premised on an exclusive view of citizenship and the rights of its citizens, including women and non-Muslims, is simply untenable. All too often, people who express the desire for an Islamic state really do not know what *shari'a* says on the subject. For them an Islamic state conjures up an idealistic notion of the Golden Age of Islam where Muslims were powerful—rather like the portrayals offered in the historical dramas and serials that are so often presented, for example, on Egyptian television (and which I notice are also frequently to be seen here on Malaysian television as well). How are the majority of Muslims ever to understand what is meant by "the historicity of Islam"—of Islamic law, politics, and the social history of its original religious revelation—when their ideas of the subject are so largely influenced by these expensively produced but simplistic fantasies?

But those same enthusiasts for the establishment of an Islamic state have little notion of what *shari'a* really means and what its implications are: for their everyday lives and lifestyle, for character and tone of their daily existence, for ordinary human and social existence in substantial and concrete terms. In the *shari'a*, as a modern Muslim understands it, there are many positive ideas and lessons to be drawn and constructive precedents to call upon. But those of us who understand *shari'a*, its evolution and formulation historically must also recognise that there are limits to what *shari'a*, as it has existed until now, has envisaged and to what it may be invoked to endorse.

Take, for example, the issue of the rights of women. Not only is equality not envisaged by the *shari'a*, but women's access to public office and public life are generally precluded. While the socialisation of women in a society governed by the *shari'a* and the processes by which women are conditioned into a helpless, submissive, dependent existence may vary from one setting to another, little encouragement is to be found in this range of variation. Even the most progressive and enlightened interpretations of the views towards women, their social role and rights that are found within *shari'a*—as it has been understood until now—are for me simply unacceptable. They are unacceptable to me as a Muslim, not from a secular but from an Islamic point of view.

As for the rights of non-Muslims and their place in an Islamic state, conventional *shari'a* views are again disappointing. Those, again, who invoke the image of some idealised Golden Age often recall the so-called constitution of Medina as their model. Yet they offer as unproblematic and entirely adequate for all modern contingencies various precedents which are altogether limited. Within conventional *shari'a* understandings, non-Muslims who are non-believers are scarcely persons at all—if our notion of a person entails that as individuals they are bearers of rights. According to *shari'a* sources, there are believers and others. The former fall into two categories: Muslims and believing non-Muslims (who include both Christians and Jews as well as Zoroastrians). These believing non-Muslims are regarded as *dhimmi* who have some protection but not rights of equal citizenship. (Living within the Islamic polity, they enjoy its protection; but since they are neither expected nor can they really be trusted to participate in its military defence, they are subject instead to payment of a special tax or levy [the *jizyah*] in lieu of military service.) As for the non-believers, they count for even less. Having no scripture, animists, for example, are not "people of the book". They are not perceived as prospective permanent residents and, even if permitted residents on a short-term basis, they enjoy only very limited protection and rights within the "abode of Islam" or in an Islamic state.

Reformation, polemics and options for constructive action

Despite the inapplicability or the unrealisable character of conventionally understood *shari'a* today, Muslims who stand opposed on various issues all have to deal with the two imperatives of change referred to earlier: they must simultaneously maintain their Muslim religious and spiritual authenticity while seeking to understand and actualise Islam in appropriately contemporary forms.

Muslim secularists—those who do not wish to engage in any internal Islamic discourse—will have to deal with the realities of their societies where Islam is dominant: where the language of public discourse, the symbolism, and the images of culture and tradition are grounded in Islamic history and experience. If they fail to do that, they will alienate their constituencies and be dismissed as irrelevant: as secularists who have abandoned the field to the most regressive and reactionary elements within that tradition. Those who engage in serious Islamic discourse with a commitment to Islam as *shari'a* will also have to respond to the challenge of modernity. We now live in a complex, interdependent world and, in it, within nation-states which along a variety of dimensions are pluralistic—ethnically, culturally, religiously, intellectually and often also politically. Those realities cannot be ignored but must be acknowledged. The challenge is to engage with them from within an authentically Islamic perspective that is both religiously legitimate and appropriately modern.

To illustrate the dilemma that we face here I turn to a specific experience—my own experience and that of many of others who are trying to present a very different view of what Islam means and how it should be lived today. Specifically, what is of interest here is the reaction that we often encounter from others. In the mid-East a so-called secularist would say to us that to engage in Islamic discourse is a dangerous thing, implying that to do so entails making unacceptable or damaging concessions to the opponents in the field. Any such engagement requires them to adopt certain concepts, terms and methodology as well as a mode of discourse of which—of whose history and sources—secularists know very little. So they seek instead to stay away from any Islamic discourse. When novel or unconventional yet constructively modern reinterpretations of the *Qur'an* are suggested and when one challenges the sources of the *sunna*—questioning what the *sunna* meant in its originating historical context—secularist Muslims tend to offer a characteristic response. In what is clearly a correct observation, they say that the whole question of reinterpretation is so vague, elusive and controversial that every person can produce a different interpretation from a different source. This openness, they assert, is inherent in the subject matter. Interpretations differ greatly, since the ambiguity in the Islamic tradition is very large. The observation itself is correct, but as a response to the question of the urgency of Qur'anic reinterpretation it is unsatisfactory.

On the other hand, there are also those who engage in Islamic discourse on a specific, narrow understanding of what the sources are and what they mean. They exclusively and categorically claim that there can only be a single understanding of what the *Qur'an* and *sunna* mean. But between these two position lies one that is difficult, but it alone provides modern Muslims with the possibility of moving forward into the future and embracing modernity with their religious, spiritual and cultural identity intact. That is the position which takes our Islamic religion, our cultural legacy and historical heritage seriously, but does so by treating it critically—with the full force of our divinely bestowed human reason.

Since coming to Malaysia, I have encountered this same phenomenon, the same polarity. Some people here appear to be on one side of the issue and others on the other. Some dismiss as irrelevant or as too problematic all Islamic discourse, proposing instead a total secularisation or modernisation process, while others assert that we cannot do without *shari'a*, insisting as part of their claim that *shari'a* has always existed and still continues to exist in one standard form.

Whatever our stands, we need to be informed of each other's positions and their basis. In serious and open dialogue with one another, we need to make our various positions "discursively redeemable": that is, to engage together, across our differences, in a process of reasoning about and thereby clarifying the underlying presuppositions of our various positions and approaches, of why we adhere to them, and on what principled intellectual grounds we feel entitled to prefer our own positions over those of our different dialogue partners. We need to respond to one another's underlying concerns and anxieties. After all, both sides are insecure. Both feel threatened by the positions of the other and are ill-informed about each other. In countries like Malaysia and the Sudan, there are also others—especially non-Muslims—who are concerned, and with good reason, about the prospect of a *shari'a*-based Islamic state. Muslims, all of us, should also be sensitive to the reasons for their apprehensions over calls for the establishment of a *shari'a* state.

Here I use the expression "*shari'a* state" and not "Islamic state". There can be a difference, and an important one. One the one hand, there is the *shari'a* as it is conventionally understood: given, immutable, eternal. Associated with it is a regressive, nostalgic and altogether premodern notion of the state. But on the other, we can articulate a modern understanding of *shari'a* and, with it, a modern conception of an Islamic state that is appropriate to today's pluralistic, interdependent world and capable of responding to the competing imperatives of change. One understanding of *shari'a* and the Islamic state is a dead-end, the other a highway leading to open possibilities. We can choose between them. By choosing well, we can enable ourselves not only to meet the legitimate concerns of women and non-Muslims but also to resolve constructively the underlying tensions that generally, until now, have been historically characteristic of Muslim social and political existence.

Reference

Abdullahi Ahmed An-Nai'm, *Toward an Islamic Reformation: Civil Liberties, Human Rights, and International Law*. Syracuse, NY: Syracuse University Press, 1990.

3

Reformation of Shari'a or Contesting the Historical Role of the Ulama?

*Chandra Muzaffar**

I agree with Abdullahi that there is an urgent need to reform certain aspects of the *shari'a*. It is important to reiterate that Abdullahi wants *shari'a* reform to take place within the ambit of the *Qur'an* and the authentic *sunna*.

Islam: Dynamism and stagnation

Many other Muslim reformers have also called for the reconstruction of the *shari'a* along the same lines. In the last 300 years, outstanding thinkers such as Shah Walliyullah, Jamaluddin Al-Afghani, Muhammad Iqbal, Kalam Azad, Ali Shariati, Fazlur Rahman and Mohamed Arkoun have argued for the reformulation of various Islamic laws and practices so that the genuine spirit and character of the *Qur'an* would re-emerge. Great *sufi* mystics in earlier periods of Muslim history were also deeply concerned about what they saw as the decline of Islam's commitment to justice and its egalitarian values. Even the illustrious *ulama* of the

* Dr. Chandra Muzaffar's remarks in this chapter were offered as the first of two responses to Dr. Abdullahi An-Na'im's keynote address on the historicity of *shari'a* and the legitimacy of continuing evolution and reform in Islamic legal systems.

first two or three centuries were acutely conscious of the importance of formulating laws which reflected the spirit of the *Qur'an.* In a sense, it was Sayyidina Umar Ibn Khatab himself—the second caliph of Islam—who set the example by adopting policies which emphasised the essence of the Qur'anic message of justice and equality instead of merely sticking to established rules and regulations.

However, the dynamic humanitarian spirit represented by Umar and the other rightly-guided caliphs in the first thirty years or so of Islam did not last long. With the ascendancy of Muawiyah and the rise of the Umayyads Islam began to undergo a gradual change. Muawiyah established a monarchical system. He created a feudal political structure. His primary concern was the expansion of his power. Justice was secondary to him. The desire to preserve and perpetuate power at all costs resulted in the development of a political and legal system which sought to exercise maximum control over people—the *umma.* Control demands laws; it requires rules. Some of the *ulama* aided and abetted Muslim monarchs in their endeavour to enhance their power. These *ulama* provided both legality and legitimacy to feudal rule.

Certain other important developments in Muslim history strengthened this conservative, feudal ethos. Waves of Tartar invasions in the 12th and 13th centuries C.E. destroyed the famous centres of Muslim learning and culture and created a cautious, timid mood within Muslim communities—a mood not hospitable towards novel ideas, one less inclined towards experimentation and innovation but more towards conserving what was left of Islamic civilisation. By challenging Muslim identity and integrity, as it had never been challenged before, Western colonial domination from the 16th century C.E. onwards also reinforced religious conservatism and habitual political support for any prevailing *status quo.* If anything, continuing Western control over Muslim lands and resources, and Muslim helplessness *vis-à-vis* Palestine and other traumas, have persuaded sections of the Muslim *umma* that their survival depends upon their ability to preserve Muslim identity through rigid adherence to dogma and doctrine.

Islam, ulama and conservatism

It is this conservatism, particularly pronounced in the case of theological matters, which the present-day Muslim world has inherited from the past. The *ulama* reflect this conservatism. Indeed, more than any other group within the *umma*, it is the *ulama* who are largely responsible for impeding all attempts at reconstructing aspects of the *shari'a*. Because the *ulama* refuse to adopt an evaluative attitude towards the *shari'a* as it has evolved through time, the *umma* as a whole also evinces an uncritical stance towards Islamic law. This is a measure of the overpowering grip of the *ulama* upon the Muslim mind.

Why are the *ulama* so influential? There are perhaps two interrelated reasons. The *ulama* are seen by the vast majority of the *umma* as the protectors of Islamic tradition. More specifically, they are seen as the protectors of the *Qur'an*, the word of God, and the *sunna*, the way of the Prophet Muhammad s.a.w. In addition, their piety and their knowledge of Arabic and theology enhance their standing. For the *umma*, the *ulama* are the unquestionable, almost infallible, authority on anything and everything connected with Islam.

Unfortunately, the *umma* does not realise that while the *ulama* have preserved the sanctity of the *Qur'an*, their injunctions and judicial pronouncements (*fatwa*) are not always in accordance with the actual teachings of the *Qur'an* or even the authentic *sunna*. In fact, on a variety of issues ranging from political authority and international relations to the rights of women and the position of non-Muslim minorities, the *ulama* are bound much more by rules and regulations enshrined in the *shari'a* as they understand it than by the *Qur'an* or the *sunna*. But the *umma*, often ignorant of these important distinctions, are uncritically loyal to the authority of the *ulama*.

The power of the *ulama* is also derived from yet another source—or perception. They are perceived by a substantial segment of the *umma* as the true defenders of the faith during its critical moments in history. Undeniably, in facing the colonial onslaught, especially upon religion and culture, many of the *ulama* played a crucial role, not simply of resistance but of preservation. It was largely due to their unwavering commitment to the religion and to their sacrifice that Islam retained its pre-eminent position as the faith and the way of life of the people.

Any attempt to reform Islamic laws and practices should accordingly begin with an open acknowledgement of the role of the *ulama* in protecting tradition and defending the faith. Whatever stance they may adopt now or in the future, in the past they have played an important historical role. The *ulama* should be honoured and respected for their contribution to Islam and Muslim civilisation. Nonetheless, elements in the *shari'a* which they have preserved as sacred should be reformulated in line with the *Qur'an* and in the interest of the *umma* itself.

Shari'a reform: The position of women

In seeking to reform the *shari'a,* we should draw upon resources which are integral to Muslim identity and the Islamic tradition. Reforms which are rooted in identity and tradition have a better chance of being accepted by the *umma.* For instance, while conservative groups may want to give exclusive emphasis to a woman's identity as daughter, wife and mother, those of us who value a woman's public role can choose to draw the attention of the *umma* to the position of Queen Balqis in the *Qu'ran.* It is significant that the *Qur'an* lauds her competence and ability as head of state. Similarly, if champions of patriarchy point to polygamy as an accepted practice in the Prophet's time, the advocates of sexual equality can bring to the notice of both Muslim men and women the little known fact that the Prophet forbade his son-in-law Ali from taking a second wife because it would not be just to Fatima (Ali's wife and the Prophet's daughter). This is also part of the Prophet's tradition.

What is important is that, in selecting examples connected to Islamic identity and tradition, one must be guided by the holistic, integrated vision of life and living embodied in the *Qur'an.* This means that one should not emphasise only those aspects which serve one's purpose, while ignoring or minimising other elements in the *Qur'an.* Thus, while women's groups recognise the role of both women and men as *khalifah Allah* (vicegerent of God), with all the responsibilities and rights that are thereby entailed, they should not forget that the *Qur'an* also acknowledges the importance of the woman's position as mother. Likewise, while justice for the female is given the importance it deserves in the *Qur'an,* the holy Book also advises women—and men—to be modest and chaste.

Women should not view values such as modesty and chastity and their roles as wife and mother as backward or retrogressive. Certain dimensions of the crisis in male-female relationships and the family in the West reflect, and make us realise, the significance of some of the eternal values and roles that the *Qur'an* espouses. There is no doubt that, taken as a whole, the *Qur'an* has a far more balanced vision of the woman than contemporary Western civilisation offers.

Using the *Qur'an* in particular as their framework, Muslim women should be able to develop their role as *khalifah Allah* and, in the process, transform Muslim civilisation itself. As they become aware of the rights assured them by the *Qur'an*, more and more women are demanding a bigger role in society. This is happening even in such ultra-conservative societies as Kuwait and Saudi Arabia.

Women, I am convinced, will play a significant role in the reformulation of values and the reconstruction of attitudes in the Muslim world, and will thereby bring those values and attitudes closer to the genuine spirit of the *Qur'an*. More than the other sex, women have a direct, vested interest in the reinterpretation of what passes for Islamic principles and practices. For that reason, they will fight to re-establish the true meaning of Islam. When that happens, the attitude and outlook towards Islam itself, of Muslims and among people of other religions, will undergo a profound transformation.

Every social transformation in history requires a social force to carry it forward. The transformation of the Muslim world—who knows?—might be brought about by women. *Insha'Allah.*

4

Islamic Reform, Muslim Law and the Shari'a State

*Asma Larif-Béatrix**

Before highlighting the major ideas in Abdullahi's talk—ideas which are basic to every serious project of Islamic reform—we should remember that *islah* or Islamic reformation has been *the* issue, the central concern, within the Muslim world since Napoleon's expedition to Egypt in 1798-1799. The need for an effective response, a productive adjustment, to new challenging times has been felt by Muslims everywhere. But the diagnoses and remedies that have been offered in the various Muslim countries to overcome former weaknesses and decadence have differed, giving rise to a variety of social and political movements.

Idealisation of the past

Underlying these variations, however, is to be found a main set of common ideas concerning *islah* which have crossed space and time without noticeable alteration. These core ideas attribute all the shortcomings and travails experienced by Muslim societies

* Dr. Asma Larif-Béatrix's commentary was offered as the second response to Dr. Abdullahi An-Nai'im's opening address. The author expresses her thanks to Norani Othman and to Clive Kessler, for helping her to clarify the argument of this commentary and for improving its presentation in English.

throughout history, and especially in modern or recent times, to the departures made by Muslims of succeeding generations from the authentic and authoritative path of Islam traced by the Prophet and his companions. The way to catch up with modern technology and to throw off foreign domination, these core ideas accordingly suggest, is simply to return to the purity of Islam in its founding form: by reinstating God's divine law, following the *sunna* of his Prophet, and by emulating the original and incorruptible Muslim state that was constructed and headed by the Prophet in Medina.

This prescription—this idealisation as an eternally valid paradigm of Islam's founding moment and of the sociopolitical structures that were fashioned at the time—not only condemns as error, deviation, even heresy, all that fourteen subsequent centuries of Islamic civilisation yielded. It also ignores historical facts. Following the Prophet's death a succession of disputes, political plots and assassinations ensued, and the Muslim state remained largely unrealised, far from achieving any stabilised form or even being effectively shaped. Why, then, the persistent idealisation of former times to which today's Muslims are persistently subjected? Here we come to what Abdullahi terms "anachronistic projections".

The historicity of Islam and Muslim historical attitudes

Muslim societies, and those who today seek to fashion their future, need to develop an adequate historical attitude towards, and understanding of, their own past. If history is nothing more than a screen for the projection of our collective fantasies, then all the social arrangements and political constructs established on the weak or even illusory foundation of those wishful projections are doomed to failure, even devastating collapse.

An honest historical attitude is not only an intellectual necessity. It is also a practical political requirement for Muslims seeking to offer solutions that have some plausible prospects of success to the enormous political, economic and social problems now affecting their societies. A cool and enquiring view of history, though it will always yield understandings that are provisional and incomplete, does make it possible for us to see as humanly constructed and therefore as historically contingent things that are all too often though improperly treated as absolute. It can, for example, enable us to question the often asserted divine character, not of the inspiration of the *shari'a* but of the particular historical forms—both intellectual or textual and also legal-institutional—in which throughout history the *ulama* gave expression in their own times and way to that revelatory inspiration.

The human character and history of shari'a

For Muslims whose thinking is shaped by the ideas of *islah* no less than for those of quite traditional outlook, the *shari'a* and Islamic jurisprudence generally have an absolute character. They are seen as not merely amplifying the *Qur'an* and *sunna* but also, on that account, as actually sharing in some overall or pervasive way the divine or sacred character of their founding textual and prophetic inspiration. The product of that human and historical process of elaboration—the great and impressive intellectual tradition of Islamic legal culture, as it was developed by many of the best minds within Islamic civilisation over fourteen centuries—is denied its human character. Misattributing this central product of the intellectual vitality of Islamic civilisation to divine origin not only dishonours the humans whose accomplishment it was. It also heretically attributes to God what is the achievement of mere mortals. But if the *shari'a* is the work of mere mortals—some of the most learned and intellectually gifted mortals of Muslim history—how can it be held by Muslims of good conscience to be, in all its realised and amplified details, divine?

Abdullahi's analysis highlights the largely human character of the *shari'a*, as a humanly produced historical construction. Looking at the matter in a strictly chronological fashion, he reminds us, the view that Islamic jurisprudence (that is, the four main juristic schools or *madhab*) evolved upon the basis of an already fixed and verifiable *sunna* is untenable. To his argument a further point might be added: that the *sunna* was not only codified more than two centuries after the Prophet's death but that, when it was, its interpretation was at the time also framed within certain again historically conditioned mental or intellectual limits.

Language constraints and textual literalism

According to Jabiri, a Moroccan scholar, Muslim history witnessed in the years between 150–300 *hijri* a period of intensive codification, as many leading Muslim societies shifted their primary emphasis from an oral to written tradition. During this crucial historical period of transition away from oral primacy, the bedouin came to be regarded—nostalgically, and perhaps paradoxically—by the *ulama*, by grammarians and by literate people generally as cultural paragons: as an uncorrupted source of Arabic grammar, pronunciation, interpretation and the like. The consequent fixation or crystallization of the Arabic language within the mental framework or horizons of bedouin culture had the effect of restricting the interpretive possibilities of Muslim jurisprudence. Hence, despite the richness of the available Arabic vocabulary, Jabiri demonstrates, it has been difficult for legal reasoning to free itself from and go beyond limits that are embedded within and imposed by that archaising vocabulary itself.

An initial break with the tyranny of the letter—of an unwarranted textual literalism—can be made if we refrain, as we are entitled to and an adequate historical understanding requires, from asserting that *shari'a* and Islam are one and the same thing. This last idea, advanced by Abdullahi towards the end of his analysis, is neither heretical nor disrespectful. Rather, properly understood it can generate a humble attitude towards the *Qur'an* and the Prophet's *sunna*. Meanwhile, the *shari'a*, as intended by various *ulama* and *fuqaha*, has been and continues to be implemented in a number of Muslim societies. Yet this implementation of what Muslim legal scholars had developed and understood as *shari'a* did not prevent and still fails to deter poverty, injustice, corruption or political instability. The Islamic message that is embedded within the *Qur'an*—and, from that source, is so widely scattered and refracted via human interpretation throughout the often opportunistically fashioned *sunna*—should disturb rather than calm the questing Muslim conscience, especially in our own challenging times.

Part II:

Islam and the Modern Nation-State

5

The Muslim State: Pursuing a Mirage?

*Asma Larif-Béatrix**

Introduction

In some Muslim countries, the opposition between those who are for a Muslim state and those who are against it can degenerate at any time into civil war. Anathemas and accusations are exchanged daily. "You are dissolute unbelievers bound and subjugated by the West, and we intend to liberate you by rebuilding the incomparably good, moral, and progressive Muslim state and society", says one side. "You are the forces of darkness and reaction, totalitarians and fascists who hide yourselves behind Islam", the other side replies. And sometimes, alas, the two come to blows, and even kill. It is noteworthy that, in their struggle, both sides place great emphasis upon the state: one wants to maintain and consolidate its secular character, the other to erase and eradicate it.

In our time, more than ever, the relationship between the state and religion in Muslim societies requires profound yet calm

* The text published here is a revised version of that which opened the symposium's second part on "Islam and the Modern Nation-State". The author thanks Clive Kessler for his advice in clarifying the argument and improving its presentation in English.

analysis. Many parts of the Muslim world are now experiencing an increasing demand, especially after the Iranian revolution, for the establishment of an Islamic state. This impulse is largely shaped by the determination to overcome a frustrating legacy of Western political and economic domination and to give birth to a more egalitarian society. Yet this high-minded motivation must not prevent us from questioning the central idea of a Muslim state. My aim in doing so is not to make a choice for others, only to draw attention to the danger of hastily subscribing to any ideology which may choose to label itself Islamic. Indeed, before arguing about something, we must first ascertain whether it even exists, or ever could.

In order to examine as dispassionately as possible so impassioned an issue, we need to address two cardinal questions:

- What are the institutional bases and historical roots of the state in Muslim societies? and,

- What is said and what left unsaid about the relationship between the *shari'a* and the state?

The institutional bases and historical roots of the state

When we examine the major sources of *shari'a* law, seeking to extract from them the institutional bases for an Islamic state or even any state at all, we are forced to admit that there is nothing there to build upon. No premise for a theory of the state is to be found either in the *Qur'an* or in the *shari'a,* both of which deal with society rather than the state. Studying the *shari'a* therefore leaves us with an ever more troubling question: why, in the face of its silence on the question, does Muslim thinking persistently remain so deeply obsessed with the state?

The *Qur'an* is considered the primary source of *shari'a* law, and some even urge its adoption as the constitution of the modern state. But what constitution can we extract from the *Qur'an*? As is well known, only a very few of its more than six thousand verses deal with law and society, and fewer still with the state. And they do so only remotely, we must hasten to add, because those verses are so vague and imprecise. Take, for example, the Qur'anic verse [*an-Nisa* 4:62] which states that a Muslim must be obedient to God, to the Prophet, and to those who hold authority. What kind of authority does the *Qur'an* refer to here? To the authority that reposes in the ruler? In the *ulama*? Or partly in both of them, but, if so, how should we proceed should the two happen not to agree with each other? Who should have the last word? Who can decide about peace and war? Who may abrogate an existing law or introduce a new one in situations of crisis or emergency? How is power to be transmitted ? And so on ... No answer is to be found to any of these questions in the *Qur'an* itself.

Searching the further sources of the *shari'a* for guidance concerning the state proves no more successful. The main problems with the second source of Islam, the *sunna*, concern its authenticity and the historical conditions of its collection, especially in its political aspects. No collections of *hadith* were assembled during the Prophet's own lifetime. Why, we may well wonder, were the *hadith* collected only some three centuries after his death, and why, when they were finally compiled, were they assimilated to the *Qur'an* and "rationalised" in accordance with rigid pre-existing categories which continued to ignore the state?

The third source of *shari'a* is learned consensus or *ijma*, though, having noted it, we must also immediately note the ironic lack of consensus about *ijma* itself and its conditions, even among the narrow circles of the *ulama* themselves. The validation of an *ijma* requires, for some, the agreement of only a few but, for others, the agreement of the whole body of *ulama* from the entire Muslim world. In practice, and because the Muslim world does not have the equivalent of an organised church, there of course never has been any consensus among the *ulama*. The necessarily fictive character of *ijma* apparently did not escape Ibn Hanbal, founder of the Hanbali school, who is said to have remarked that "whoever states *ijma* is a liar". As for the prime object of our interest here, namely the state, an *ijma*—for example on the way a ruler is to be designated and succeeded—was never applied, even during the time of the four rightly-guided caliphs.

The fourth source of the *shari'a* is *qiyas* or analogy, although it is not recognised by all the Muslim juristic schools. And again specifically, as for the state and its institutions, here too, we once more find, there is nothing to build upon. Take, for example, the *qiyas* that was made by the *ulama* in the political field when, after having deputized for the Prophet during his final illness, Abu Bakar was on that basis subsequently designated after the

Prophet's death as his political successor and leader of the Muslim community. This decision was based on the assertion of a general analogy between *"al imama al-sughra"* (direction of the prayer) and *"al-imama al-kubra"* (succession to the caliphate). Clearly, this eliding together of the two *imama* is drawn upon a single instance and is based merely upon a superficial similarity, on outward or descriptive appearances, not on any substantial principle or intrinsic grounds. Or again, consider the *qiyas* made by Al-Ashari (A.H. 260-324/C.E.874-935) between the contract of marriage and the *bay'ah* or contract of allegiance to the ruler. As the validity of the former contract required two witnesses, so too, it was reasoned, would the second require the authenticating presence of two *ulama* (see Laoust 1983: 130). Once more, the resemblance which provides the basis for this piece of analogical reasoning is metaphorical, not substantive. For some Muslim thinkers, *qiyas* is anyway a dangerous method, being constructed as it is on a conception of homogenous social time that denies the historicity of human society and its institutions (see Arkoun 1970).

The fifth source of *shari'a* is the *furu*, or those various other elements of law which constitute subsidiary sources of Muslim jurisprudence. These include, for example, *istihsan*, which means the adoption of a juridical decision out of necessity or public interest, such as keeping in prison a person suspected of theft. This position was apparently defended by the Maliki school yet rejected by the Hanafi because, it is said, according to Abu Hanifa it is better to release a guilty person than to harm an innocent one. Or again, take the question whether it is permissible to sacrifice an innocent individual to save the group, or a smaller group to ensure the survival of a larger. For its part the Shafe'i school does not recognise *istihsan* even in principle, claiming that "he who practises *istihsan* improperly substitutes himself for God, the supreme legislator". The *furu* also included customs covering some extensive areas of economic life such as contracts. These provided everyday transactions with a conveniently supple or flexible frame, but at the expense of wider legal consistency and unity. And, within all this, what is said about the state? Absolutely nothing.(1)

Why, then, in view of this resounding silence of the sources of Islamic law on questions of state structure are many Muslims so obsessed by the idea of a Muslim state? Why, when urging its establishment, do its advocates ignore this complete absence of any juridical foundation or justification for the state within canonical

Islam? Puzzling and even paradoxical, this insistence on its importance seems necessarily entailed by the interplay of two contrary impulses: the compelling need of Muslims for a state, a structure of integration different from and superseding the tribal; and their simultaneous and quite fundamental fear that, once created, such a structure might escape their control. This point requires some extended consideration.

State and shari'a: The "said" and the "unsaid"

To speak of the state, society, the economy or the intellectuals (and so on) implies that each of these institutions has its own space or field of activity, separate from the others. Never clear-cut, this separation or construction of fields of activity is always partial or relative. In Europe, for example, the state fought the church to gain its autonomy, taking hundreds of years to do so, and even then rather incompletely. In the same way, the intellectual field also had to struggle to free itself from political and economic pressures and to acquire its own measure of autonomy. Though it can never be completely autonomous, the very existence of any space of specialised activity implies a minimum of liberty, a modicum of sovereignty.

In the same way again, the state too needs its own space which becomes vital as soon as society evolves beyond the tribal stage. Yet this necessary space is not granted to the state in Muslim thinking. Hence the absence of any Muslim theory of the state: that whose existence is not recognised need not be theorised. Muslim thinking has denied not merely the existence, but with it therefore also the sovereignty, of the state. Instead, it is the *shari'a* which enjoys overriding preeminence in Muslim sociopolitical thought. Elevated as God's supreme and sole law, the *shari'a* becomes the most effective weapon imaginable against any claim for sovereignty or autonomy arising from the political field. This follows from what the notion of autonomy necessarily entails. Every autonomous institution must enjoy to some degree the capacity to create its own laws, its own ethic, and its own project. It is precisely this requirement that has never been accepted, at least in principle or theoretically, by Muslim thinkers: by those who refused to compromise or diminish in any way their attachment to the absolute ascendancy of the *shari'a*.

The stateless tradition of Arabian society in which Islam was born together with Islam's strict monotheism combined to limit the state, its claims and legitimacy. The reluctance of a free bedouin society to become entangled within the mesh of the state is easily understood. But to understand the similar wariness towards the state of the urban religious thinkers requires that we grasp the thoroughgoing or absolutist character of their monotheism.

For insistently monotheistic Muslims such as Ashari, the unity and transcendance of God left no room for any delegation or devolution of authority to human beings. Pushed to its extreme, Ashari's monotheism not only denies all autonomy to the state and society, out of the fear of associating any partners to God or any conjoint legislators to the supreme legislator. More, it also refuses to recognise any necessary relation between cause and effect. Such an extreme monotheism insists instead that, when something that is thrown into the air falls down again, this occurs not because nature possesses its own laws but because God intervenes every time to make that object fall down again. However, we need not go to such absolutist extremes in upholding the principle of monotheism. The unity and transcendance of God can also be differently but equally well understood in another way: because God is unique and transcendent no human action, no exercise of necessarily partial human autonomy, could possibly impugn his transcendance, and no natural law created by him could ever diminish his sovereignty.

Yet we are left with a question. The Muslim tradition, it is argued above, lacked any theory of the state, refusing to acknowledge its existence and to provide any space for its development. How, then, is the fact to be explained that Muslim states did not merely exist but flourished, bequeathing at the height of their power and prosperity the image of a fully developed civilisation?

Here we must bear in mind two main points. First, that the Islamised areas outside Arabia already had their own very strong traditions of government: the Egyptian, Babylonian, and Sassanid to name but a few. It was through these already existing institutions, and with the help of new converts who were highly skilled in the art of administration, that Muslims established their governance over various conquered and Islamised countries.

Second, we should not forget that throughout Islamic history state builders, while maintaining the fiction of an Islamic state, imposed themselves upon society by force. In effect, the claims of *raison d'état* escaped from the control of the *ulama*, ceasing to be part of their ethic or ideological preserve, their rhetoric or strategic repertoire. It passed instead to those who might themselves wield and act upon such a concept of *realpolitik*. Although it was never theoretically accepted, a *de facto* separation between *syasa* (policy) and *shari'a* emerged and, even contrary to doctrinal assertions, a significant historical evolution was thereby set in motion: what might be called the political abdication of the *ulama*. Once the *ulama* had surrendered their claims upon policy in favour of preserving their ideal view and their own custodianship of the *shari'a*, the very emphasis on the *shari'a* law as a way to control the state made possible and eventually culminated in its use by the state to control society. This paradoxical and often unrecognised historical reversal must be kept in mind in all discussions, including the debates of our times, concerning the idea of a Muslim state limited by the *shari'a*.

This historically conditioned incapacity to conceptualise adequately the state, its autonomy and logic is responsible for what may be termed the utopian Muslim state.

The Islamic utopia: Reality or ideal, attainable objective or mirage?

With the dynastic consolidation of the Ummayad caliphate (A.H.41-132/C.E.661-750) and even before it, the idea of a lost perfect political system appeared that still dominates, even haunts, the Muslim imagination. No theorist of the state pointed out more sharply than Ibn Khaldun the dramatic oscillation in Islamic history between the utopian state and its historical implementation.

Not confined merely to mundane authority (*mulk*, or royal power), the institution of the caliphate according to Ibn Khaldun did not outlast the four rightly-guided caliphs. It ended with them; thereafter we encounter only the unholy desire to win power and to keep it. From its inception, every project of state-building and consolidation accordingly displays a distinct combination of features. Prominent among them are:

- a religious ideology based on the purity of the pristine Islamic message that stresses, *inter alia*, the unity of God, a strict egalitarianism among the believers, and a mandatory purity of behaviour;

- a leader strongly linked to his followers; and finally
- a militaristic religious organisation.

Consisting from its outset of a leader and only a handful of followers, this initial group succeeds in attracting through its religious appeal *(da'wa)* a broad coalition of dissatisfied people, transcending the diverse causes of their discontent. When this leader eventually considers his group sufficiently strong to challenge the government, he stages an armed insurrection. At this stage, two scenarios are possible: if the established political system still remains strong, it seeks to contain this new force, coopting it to its own cause; in the other case, the existing political order is overthrown, replaced by that of the insurgents.

But, as Ibn Khaldun points out, the state's political stability is not easily assured. No political system can ever resist the effects of an endemic tension, a recurrent internal dynamic: the deterioration of its inner spirit of cohesiveness and the degeneration of the religious ideology on which the regime first consolidated itself. The very nature of the state inescapably leads to hierarchy, to the assertion of a royal hereditary principle eclipsing its founding egalitarianism, while the regime is soon impelled to seek autonomy, especially autonomy from the original group of supporters responsible for its initial establishment. Four generations allow sufficient time for a new challenger to emerge: to provide him with his pretext to seize power and his opportunity to seek the regeneration of a by now corrupt state and society.

This recurrent process clearly demonstrates that the Islamic utopian state is powerful at only two stages in this cycle: its appeal is potent in the initial process of state-formation and consolidation and in the final phase of its collapse or destruction. Between these two moments, the ideology collapses or retreats. In its place, the real rather than the imagined state now presents itself, confronting us with its own distinct, if in this context quite unrecognised and untheorised, logic.

This quite schematic survey of the Khaldunian state-building cycle poses a significant question concerning the nature of the Muslim state. Is it the political entity that exists in some particular historical form, or is it that existing reality's idealised self-representation, the form that it takes in its own imagination, its utopia? Is the much discussed Muslim state, in short, the political entity which may have existed at any time in history; or is that entity instead only the imperfect, contingent, and historically realised form of an ideal which is itself the purported reality of the Muslim state?

Should we wish to affirm the former possibility, we must also accept at least two further ideas entailed by it: first, that whether just or despotic, all of the states that were formed after the four rightly-guided caliphs are in fact Muslim states and are entitled to be characterised as such, simply because their leaders professed the Muslim faith and contributed to the historical development of Islamic civilisation; and second, that to be recognised as an Islamic state, a regime need not conform with some supposedly pure yet lost prototype, and that in consequence it remains free to seek its own historically and ideologically unconstrained solutions to its problems.

If, on the other hand, we adopt the second point of view and see the Muslim state as utopian—as the idealised representation of or alternative to the actual state—then we must also accept that this utopia, as some fourteen centuries of Muslim history amply demonstrate, is somehow unattainable, beyond the reach of human possibilities.

The objection might be made to the skepticism of this second position that, like myth, utopia may play a positive role in liberating the imagination and may even become part of our lives. This, of course, is true, provided that we can still distinguish between myth and reality. When they become conflated, or when the two become totally confused and the myth becomes the reality, what results is pathological behaviour. There is little of any liberating imagination to be found in what the new Muslim zealots of our own time have said and done. They merely seem to be repeating, unawares, the familiar Khaldunian pattern of insurgency against the state.

Shari'a-based regulation—of what? and by whom?

Two further points should be noted here. These concern the impact of *shari'a* law on both state and society; and the possible manipulation of the *shari'a*, or the deflection of its purposes, to constrain society rather than the state.

The impact of the *shari'a* laws on the relationship between the state and the society in Muslim countries is complex and not easy to assess. What is undeniable is that *shari'a* law has played a major role in their divorce: in the historical separation that gradually emerged between the political order and its social basis in Islamic civilisation. The rulers as well as the ruled knew, and know, that their state is based on *syasa* and *raison d'état*, not on the *shari'a* which is left with society as its proper domain. The *shari'a* becomes preoccupied with morality, not policy, as its central concern. Consequently, any sign of human weakness, especially among the rulers and the powerful, can be seized upon by any Muslim preacher, who may readily turn to some advantage any such un-Islamic behaviour. What results is mutual suspicion. In relation to society, the tendency of the state is to be harsh, though never totalitarian, while society, in its attitudes towards the state, tends to be deeply disloyal, though outwardly deferential and obedient.

Strict application of the *shari'a* laws with the intention of limiting the state, of preventing it from itself becoming a source of law, in fact results instead in the restricting of society. Faced with social and political problems, the rulers are soon tempted to contain through recourse to the *shari'a* laws not only oppositional challenges, which are always religiously tinged, but even the imagined threat of mere dissent. The rulers' motivation for the introduction of *shari'a* law in such circumstances is questionable. The unstated cynical discourse, the logic of the rulers' riposte to the threat of moral insurgency, is in effect to say: "Since you want us to be Muslims and challenge us to implement Islamic law, we shall oblige: we shall flog you, cut off your hands, and look after your morality, especially your women's morality!" Not "society against the state" here, but Muslim society intimidated by the state, through its rulers' threatened or actual recourse to the *shari'a*. A strict application of *shari'a* laws this may perhaps be, but the question is, by whom? and with what objective?

Muslims are entitled to be genuinely disappointed, even bitter, at the ends to which implementation of the *shari'a* has been turned in many countries. But, while justifiably distressed by these developments, they have been paralysed in their responses. They have been immobilised by their inability to conceive of an Islamic state without the *shari'a* and its *hudud* laws. Unable to question whether these are the indispensable essence, the *sine qua non*, of any Muslim state, they are compelled to remain silent. Despite his remotenessness in time, how near to our own experience is the example of one Muslim living under the Abassid dynasty who, on seeing a crowd gather, enquired of a bystander what was going on. "Nothing at all", he was told, "the sultan has ordered the amputation of a thief's hand". "May God be praised," he replied, "the hidden thief is cutting off the hand of the exposed one!" (Isbihy, quoted in Mehdi [1991]: 135).

Conclusion

Today, more than ever before, there is an urgent need throughout the Muslim *umma* to rethink the state and the *shari'a*, to explore their relationship outside the categories of *kufr* and *iman*. The use of these latter categories undoubtedly restricts knowledge, but without necessarily strengthening our faith. A well-founded and methodical dismantling of the existing, ready-made discourse about the *Qur'an*, the *shari'a*, and the Muslim state (and other such unquestioned and even taboo issues) might liberate the Muslim mind and Muslim history from an unwarranted and unhelpful appropriation, in the name of "orthodoxy", by an ill-informed, backward-looking, and partisan political project. There is a need to reopen questions whose long accepted closure has in the past stultified Islamic society and which, in the present, prevents us from seizing and appropriately fashioning our future. The historical period which witnessed an important acceleration in the codification of the *shari'a* was followed by the "closing the doors of *ijtihad*" and by an extreme "virilisation" of Islam—that is, of giving the Islamic tradition a predominantly masculine emphasis. However, this selective appropriation now poses new questions for us in our times. Yet if addressing these questions is to be a fruitful endeavour, if their implications are to be clearly understood, certain crucial periods in Islamic history still await their adequate historian who will at last enable us to see them clearly.

Those who are so vocal about the *shari'a* and the implementation of the *hudud* should remember that, although developed, as the *ulama* intended it, to serve as a brake upon the arbitrary power of the state, the *shari'a* in fact never served to restrain the state or limit its abuses in any way. Those who today call for the implementation of the *hudud* are therefore not simply repeating an old illusion of the *ulama*; they are actually calling for the exercise of powers whose use will actually rebound against them and Muslim society generally. They must also know that many of these repressive laws long predate Qur'anic Islam. Their traces are to be found in the Old Testament of the Bible and go back, before its times, to the laws of ancient Babylonia. We may well ask, therefore, whether the Muslim consciousness which accordingly rejects the harsh "justice" of the Arabian desert can be branded as un-Islamic.

The *Qur'an* has for so long been subjected by its scholarly guardians to an intensive and imbalanced legalism—to what may be termed a process of juridical overdevelopment or overexploitation—that we risk losing sight of its ultimate meaning and spirituality. The essential Quran'ic vision has been obscured by centuries of selective legalism, of lop-sidedly legalistic interpretation and appropriation. My own utopia consists in the liberation of Islam from its familiar and often overvalued juridical aspects, which unlike that enduring spiritual message itself—we must never forget—are merely time-bound, contingent, and historical.

Endnote

1. For further details concerning the sources of the *shari'a*, the contradictions between them, and their limits, see the interesting book by Mahdi (1991).

References

Arkoun, M., "Introduction" in *Le Coran* (trans. Kasimirski), Flammarion, Paris, 1970.

Mahdi, F., *L'Irak: Fondements et Mécanismes de l'état en Islam*, Harmattan, Paris, 1991.

Laoust, H., *Les Schismes dans l'Islam*, Payot, Paris, 1983.

6

The Islamic State and its Constitution

*Mohammad Hashim Kamali**

Introduction

Despite the absence of a clear mandate in the sources of Islam concerning the definition and attributes of an Islamic state, the view has prevailed among the *ulama* that Islam does propose a certain political order, that Islam is both a religion and state, and that these two aspects of Islam cannot be meaningfully separated from one another.

Some of the evidence that is given in support of this view is indirect and perhaps inconclusive, but it is not devoid of force. It is recognised that the Prophet s.a.w. neither appointed nor nominated a successor to lead the community after him, nor did he give any clear instruction as to the formation of a state. Nevertheless, he was himself a head of state and left behind, in his capacity as political leader, a legacy of verbal and practical instruction which the *ulama* have relied upon in expounding the basic attributes of political authority in Islam. The precedent of his first successors, the four rightly-guided caliphs, in state affairs has facilitated further elaboration of the same theme.

* Professor Hashim Kamali's analysis in this chapter was presented as the second of two main papers in the symposium's session dealing with "Islam and the Modern Nation-State".

This essay does not propose discussing the polemics of whether Islam is a religion only or both a religion and state, but investigates, in broad outline, some of the basic attributes of an Islamic polity. This is not to deny, however, the controversial nature of the continuing debate concerning the Islamic state. Ever since the proposed establishment of such a state in Pakistan and elsewhere, scholars have continued to differ on the nature and attributes of this proposition. But many have envisaged the Islamic state as a logical extension of Islam and as an instrument with which to facilitate implementation of its *shari'a.*

This is in fact the centre-piece of the whole argument in favour of establishing an Islamic state. Since Islam brought with it a legal system, the *shari'a,* it seems only logical to infer that Islam also proposes a government to enforce the *shari'a.* Any government that is committed to enforcing the law of Islam, as this discussion will elaborate, may be termed Islamic. Supportive arguments for this theme are also found in the Qur'anic concepts of *umma* and of human vicegerency or *khilafah,* in its injunction commanding good and forbidding evil, and in the Qur'anic requirement of administering justice. The concept of *khilafah,* or the vicegerency of man, is by its nature rooted in the concept of trust (*amanah*) which is also a Qur'anic principle and an attribute of political leadership in Islam. The basic unity of religion and state in Islam also represents a logical extension of *tawhid,* the oneness of Allah, which is a cardinal principle of the faith and a main feature of Islam's unitarian outlook on life.

The constitutional theory of Islam revolves around these concepts, namely *umma, shari'a, khilafah, shura* (consultation) and *bay'ah* (pledge of allegiance). This essay discusses some of these concepts as the basis for offering an attempted general characterisation of an Islamic polity. On that conceptual basis, the Islamic state is accordingly characterised as an egalitarian order which advocates simplicity and closeness to the populace; it is a welfare state with a centralised structure and authority, but one whose powers are, however, limited by reference to the *shari'a.* It is also a representative government which is accountable to the people. The Islamic state is not a theocracy; it is a civilian state which is neither sacred nor divinely ordained. These are some of the themes to be elaborated in this exposition, though this attempt at characterising the Islamic state is in no way exhaustive.[1]

Umma and state

The Arabic word for community, *umma*, is a derivative of *umm*, meaning "mother". *Umma* in Islam signifies more than the motherland. *Ummat al-Islam* comprises the entire collectivity of Muslims living anywhere regardless of their geographical location or the political boundaries separating them. *Umma* is a Qur'anic concept which was initially applied to the Islamic community of Medina.

The *Qur'an* highlights some of the attributes of *umma* as including belief in the truth of Islam, dedication to righteousness (by commanding good and forbidding evil), moderation and justice, and a single fraternity of equals.(2) Pre-Islamic Arabia did not know or use the concept of *umma*; the only form of social organisation that it knew was the tribe. Afflicted with moral, social and economic bankruptcy, pre-Islamic Arabia was therefore impressed with the morally appealing and egalitarian call of the new *umma*.(3)

With the emergence of the state of Medina, the term *umma* came to signify both religious and political unity under the leadership of the Prophet. *Umma* differed from any other preceding or succeeding community in one sense: it was an open-ended community under one universal God. This simply meant the creation for the first time in human history of a universal community based on complete equality, regardless of considerations of race, colour and ancestry.(4) Islam became not only a religion but a unifying social bond. The Prophet's declaration "that there is no merit of an Arab over a non-Arab or of a red over a black except through piety" highlighted Islam's single-minded commitment to equality.(5)

The unity that Islam proposed was meant to be for all, that is the whole of mankind. Lacking the claim or notion of a chosen people, the community kept its door open to welcome all varieties of ethnic and cultural groups. Furthermore until the onset of rapid decline under Turkish rule, Muslims throughout their territorial expansion dealt with the people of the new territories not as subjects but as citizens. This was changed, however, under the Ottoman Turks who, by exploiting and degrading their citizens, made them second-class subjects. This marked the first phase of the decline of the Islamic polity. The second phase came with European colonialism which eventually dismembered the Muslim community. Only in recent decades has there emerged a renewed awareness among Muslims who envisage their strength through unity. The ideal of the *umma* offers that potential and continues to inspire Muslims to strive toward ultimate unity.

The *umma al-Islam* may be distinguished from *dar al-Islam*. The first is centred on unity in faith, the second contemplates the legal and political aspects of a sovereign state with its territorial boundaries, population and government. A Muslim may consider himself a member of the *umma* even if he does not reside in *dar al-Islam*. This division between *dar al-Islam* and *dar al-kufr*, and the subdivision of the latter into *dar al-harb* (abode of war) and *dar al-ahd* (abode of treaty) is politically conceived and has become the focus of juristic writings, despite the absence of any mention of such divisions in the *Qur'an* or *sunna* (although there is recognition in these sources of other religions and their followers, the *ahl al-kitab*). In theory, *dar al-Islam*—which is a parallel concept to *dawlat al-Islam* (Islamic state)—comprises all territories that are totally or predominantly inhabited by Muslims and are governed by Muslim authorities. Another view, which is preferred here, maintains that it includes all territories where the *shari'a* is implemented, regardless of the religious following of their inhabitants.(6)

Umma is a Qur'anic concept but state, or *dawlah*, is not. The word *dawlah* occurs in the *Qur'an* only in the sense of material wealth. The nearest equivalent words with its political connotation that are found in the holy Book are *amr* and *hukm* which signify a "command", or a "network of command".(7) The nation-state is, of course, a Western concept representing a European phenomenon that developed between the sixteenth and seventeenth centuries C.E. It is natural therefore not to find such a concept in early Islamic political thought. Muslim jurists had much to say, however, about the body politic and the conduct of rulers and governors. If the concept of state in Europe cannot be understood in isolation from law, liberty and individualism, the Islamic concept of state cannot be understood in isolation from *umma* and *shari'a*.(8) It thus appears that the state in Islam is neither normative nor the original locus of political authority. It is perceived as a vehicle of achieving order and security in the *umma* and implementing the basic mission of Islam, that is *amr bi'l ma'ruf wa nahy 'an al-munkar* (commanding good and forbidding evil). It is the *umma*, not the state, which is the locus of political authority and the principal bearer of the Qur'anic trust of vicegerency.(9)

The population of *dawlah Islamiyyah* may include both Muslims and non-Muslims. Muslims who do not reside in the Islamic state are not necessarily or automatically citizens of that state, but residence is not a requirement of membership in the *umma*.(10)

The norm in the constitutional theory of caliphate is unity, not pluralism. This is stated in the writings of al-Mawardi (d.450/1059) and others who maintained it to be unlawful to elect more than one *imam* at the same time.(11) Only al-Baghdadi (d.403/1012) has gone on record to say that electing more than one *imam* is permissible, but only if the localities in which they are elected are divided by sea. According to the classical doctrine of caliphate, any plurality of states in the Muslim lands is necessarily anomalous and contrary to the unitarian foundation of the *umma*, which should always be the ultimate goal.(12)

The realities of contemporary world are, however, such that proposing political unity under a unified leadership and state is impractical. But if *umma* is meant to embody a religious fraternity of all Muslims that transcends the political boundaries of national states, then this has always commanded support and continues to be a reality. Despite the plurality of states and nationalities among them, Muslims are still a single *umma*. An Egyptian Muslim is Egyptian by nationality as well as a member of the Muslim *umma*. That also applies to an American Muslim who is American by nationality but relates to the *umma* as a member of Muslim fraternity.(13) Political unity is not a reality at present, but the historical model of the caliphate may perhaps be revived in a modified form, either as a federation or else in looser unity as a commonwealth of nations. (14)

Shari'a

Shari'a consists of a set of principles on morality, or dogma, as well as practical legal rules which are contained in the *Qur'an* and *sunna*. The clear injunctions, or *nusus*, of the *Qur'an* and *sunna* represent the binding corpus of the *shari'a* and it is the cardinal duty of the state in Islam to enforce them.(15) The state is a necessity in Islam if only for this purpose. Muhammad Asad observed that "the real eternal *shari'a*" consists of commands and prohibitions expressed in self-evident terms in the *Qur'an* and *sunna*. It is concise, clearly conveyed and relatively small in volume, and hence does not provide, nor was it ever intended to, detailed legislation for every contingency of life.[16] We should add to this that the *Qur'an* and *sunna* also provide a set of broad and general principles which constitute the substance of what is described as the *maqasid al-shari'a*: that is, the philosophy and objectives of *shari'a,* which are timeless and comprehensive. The concrete injunctions and the broad principles of the *Qur'an* and *sunna* embody the real eternal *shari'a.* The detailed, supplementary and additional legislation is provided through the exercise of *ijtihad*: that is, through independent reasoning which is in consonance with the spirit and principles of Islam and which aims at the realisation of *maslahah* (benefit) of the people.

Protecting the faith and implementing the law of Islam is a *raison d'être* of the *umma.* The *Qur'an* declares to this effect:

> You are the best *umma* created for mankind. You command good and you forbid evil and you believe in Allah (*al-Imran* 3: 110).

"Commanding good and forbidding evil" here means in the first place implementing the *shari'a,* although the scope of this Qur'anic concept, also known as *hisbah,* is wider than the *shari'a.* The latter part of the text explains the earlier, that is, why Allah intends it as the best *umma.*[17]

In response to a question as to the position of Islamic law in Egypt, the Egyptian scholar Muhammad Yusuf Musa writing in the early 1950s affirmed our entitlement to demand that the *shari'a* be the principal source of legislation. The Egyptian nation and its legal order, he maintained, have suffered intellectual colonialism and domination, especially from the French. But it is now time to reject such influences and return to our own heritage. We ought to encourage, Musa continued, specialised studies of *shari'a* and *fiqh* in our universities. We also need to adapt the *fiqh* to changing conditions. For it is unrealistic to expect solutions to new issues to be found in the works of the *ulama* of the past who were not faced with these questions. To support his views Musa refers to Abd al-Razzaq al-Sanhuri, who offered a positive appraisal of the value and resourcefulness of the legal heritage of Islam and its capacity for adaptation.[18]

As the main source of *shari'a,* the *Qur'an* does not embody a constitution since it does not address constitutional themes on the devolution and transfer of power or provide direction concerning other matters of state. It is rather a source whose guidance needs to be reflected and given expression in evolving state activity and legislation.(19) In that sense, Yusuf Musa is right to suggest that the *shari'a* should be designated as a principal source of legislation. The Egyptian constitution of 1973 in fact includes a provision to that effect. Similar provisions are also found in the applied constitutions of many Islamic countries.

Khilafah: The trust of vicegerency

Khilafah has two meanings, one of which is Qur'anic and refers to the vicegerency of man as the trustee of Allah on earth. *Khilafah* also refers to the institution of caliphate which was established under the four rightly-guided caliphs (*khulafa rashidun*) and continued down the centuries until its abolition by Attatürk in Turkey in early 1924. Initially, Abu Bakar and Umar, the first two caliphs of Islam, laid emphasis on the legitimacy of their leadership by resorting to *shura* (consultation), *aqd* (the contract between ruler and ruled), and *bay'ah* (an oath of allegiance).(20)

This same method was used in the appointment of their successor Othman, and the juristic elaboration of the caliphate continued to emphasise *bay'ah* and *shura*, notwithstanding the fact that in actual practice these principles were largely overlooked with the onset of a hereditary monarchy under the Ummayyads. The classical writings of al-Mawardi, Abu Yala al-Farra and Ibn Hazm are mainly concerned with the election, qualifications and duties of the caliph. The theory of caliphate also discusses the rights of the caliph and the citizen's duty of obedience to him. It speaks little of public or political rights, and discussion of the basic rights of individuals is scanty and incidental. None of these works contains a separate chapter, for example, on the fundamental rights of the citizen.(21)

The vast majority of *ulama* have held that electing an *imam* is *wajib* (obligatory) by virtue of the *ijma* (general consensus) of Prophet's companions (*sahaba*) and of succeeding generations of Muslims across the centuries. Upon the death of the Prophet the companions considered electing a succesor to him as leader as a matter of urgency, even greater than attending to his burial.(22) But to say that there must be a leader and that this is an Islamic obligation is not the same, of course, as saying that political leadership must be in conformity with any particular model.

The idea has prevailed among Muslims that there could be but one form of Islamic state, namely the form manifested under the rightly-guided caliphs. This is a common error or misconception. The truth is that Islam does not require conformity to any particular form of political structure. The Islamic state has existed historically not only in one form but many, and it is for the Muslims of every period to discover the form most suitable for their needs.[23] There is nothing in the *shari'a* to specify any particular type of political organisation. *Khilafah* and *imamah* have developed certain characteristic attributes which are generally regarded as being manifested in the Islamic concept of political leadership. However, this association is not intrinsic but historical, arising mainly as a result of the interplay of juristic doctrine and historical precedents. The political ideas and practices to which this historical association gave rise do not constitute an obligation under the *shari'a*.[24]

Government under the constitution

Neither the *shari'a* nor the juristic doctrine of Muslim scholars provides a specific pattern for the constitution of an Islamic state. Since there is no consensus on the essential features of such a state, the matter has remained open to initiative and *ijtihad*. In recent decades statesmen and scholars have produced a body of opinion from which a certain pattern seems to be emerging. But whether the emerging model of Islamic political organisation that they offer will prove persuasive throughout the *umma* remains to be seen.

The lack of any definitive paradigm of political organisation is also attributable to the absence in formative Islam of any clear source or precedent for the idea of a written constitution as the supreme law of the state. The Charter of Medina, also known as the constitution of Medina, that was enacted after the the Prophet's *hijra* to Medina may be considered as providing Muslims of later times with validating authority for the introduction of written constitutions. The question of the harmony or otherwise of any such document with the principles of Islam is of course another matter.

But despite the enactment by the Prophet of the Charter of Medina, in their own time his successors among the companions did not promulgate a written constitution, perhaps because they saw no need for one.[25] This pattern prevailed and Muslim rulers did not introduce written constitutions or a bill of rights. Apart from the ordinances of the *ulu al-amr* which addressed issues of constitutional law, constitutional matters were often regulated by reference to custom. Customary rules are naturally slow to materialise and, as one would expect, a certain degree of resistance to anomalous practices is often detectable. The founder of the Umayyad dynasty, Muawiyah was, for example, the first to appoint an heir apparent (*wali al-ahd*) and thereby validate hereditary succession. Notwithstanding the initial protest and the resistance with which it was met, a precedent was nevertheless set which was to become, by the end of the Umayyad period, a generally accepted custom. Custom thus operated as a substitute for a written constitution.[26]

To a question whether constitution-making is acceptable in Islam, Rashid Rida issued a *fatwa* answering the question in the affirmative. Since the cardinal duty of government in Islam is to implement the laws of *shari'a*, he maintained, the idea of a limited government whose powers are defined by the constitution, and of a consultative government which is committed to the ideals of justice and equality, is acceptable to Islam. If, however, the constitution contains rules which may be repugnant to the teachings of Islam, he continued, then it may be said to be misguided only with regard to its controversial elements. To substantiate this position, Rida observed that in the history of Islamic jurisprudence numerous instances are to be found where jurists have made errors in their *ijtihad* and in the books they have authored. But in such cases, we should only reject the views that are erroneous, not their endeavour in its entirety. What is not defective remains acceptable, so long as the error is corrected at an early opportunity to protect the community from deviation.[27] Mahmud Hilmy concurs with this view, commenting that there is nothing in the *shari'a* against enacting a written constitution.[28]

Commitment to equality

The Prophet and the rightly-guided caliphs left behind a legacy which was distinctly egalitarian. They had remainded close to the grass roots and avoided the pomp and ceremony practised by the

Romans and Persians. The Prophet chose simplicity and preferred to be treated as one among equals. In doing so the Prophet merely exemplified the teachings of the *Qur'an*, which insists emphatically on the equality of all believers. There is no recognition in the holy Book of any grounds of superiority of individuals or nations over one another except on the basis of moral rectitude and *taqwa*.(29)

The Prophet encouraged simplicity in both personal and public affairs. He is on record as having stated, for example, that "I am neither a king nor a tyrant",(30) and he advised his companions not to glorify anyone except Allah. In this spirit, the Prophet requested that no one should rise to stand for him upon his arrival. To the same effect, a *hadith* warns with punishment in the hereafter "those who love to be glorified by other men."(31) Again, during his last sermon in the Farewell Pilgrimage, the Prophet invited the people to claim from him any right of theirs that he might have fallen short of fulfilling, and to seek restitution for any excess in punishment or use of words by which he might have offended anyone.(32)

The companions, especially the *khulafa rashidun*, followed the Prophet's example. They, too, are known for their simplicity of style, their accessability and for not expecting their audience to stand in ceremony for them.(33) One of caliph Umar's statements, which he is said to have made upon the conquest of Iraq—that "I am not a king but a servant of Allah who is entrusted with an *amanah*"—is reminiscent of the Prophet's own insistence to the same effect.(34) Umar refused to indulge in luxury and, despite the unprecedented wealth that was accumulating during his time from conquest, he took from the *bayt al-mal* (public treasury) only what he needed for basic necessities for himself and his family. On one of his inspection tours to Sham, Umar noted signs of pomp and ceremony on the part of his governor, Muawiyah, whereupon the caliph asked, "Is this an empire that you are building [*akisrawiyyah ya Mu'wiyah*]?" Muawiyah explained that, being a neighbour to the Roman Empire, he encountered a certain level of demand for court ceremony, but the caliph was not impressed with his explanation.(35) Umar's statement concerning the *bayt al-mal* is again indicative of his principled view of the leader's relation to his community and its resources:

> My position *vis-à-vis* the public treasury is like that of a guardian in charge of the assets of orphans. I may not take anything if I am in no need, but if I am in need I may take what I need for my sustenance.(36)

Commitment to welfare

Mercy (*rahmah*), according to the Qur'anic designation, was the purpose of the Prophetic mission, and alleviation of hardship the purpose of the *shari'a*. It is therefore only befitting that the Islamic state should strive toward the realisation of mercy through *shari'a* principles. Islam proposes a welfare state as is evident from the overall emphasis in the *Qur'an* and *sunna* on helping the helpless, the needy and the poor. As a pillar of the faith *zakah* is prescribed in the *Qur'an* with the specific purpose of ensuring necessary social assistance.(37) Satisfaction of the basic requirements of those who are in need, Muslims or others, is one of the main purposes for which state revenues, whether from *zakat* or other taxes and charities, are to be expended. The Prophet himself as head of state clearly indicated that the state is committed to this purpose.

It is reported that, when the Prophet's daughter, who was married to Ali, asked her father if she could be provided with a servant for home help, the Prophet declined her request, stating

> By Allah, I shall not grant this while the ahl al-Suffah (a group of indigent *muharijun* [recent emigrants from Mecca] who for lack of shelter had to sleep in the mosque) suffer from hunger and I do not find enough to feed them.(38)

Other *hadith* can be quoted endorsing the Prophet's support for the welfare functions of the state:

> He whom God has made an administrator over the affairs of Muslims but remains indifferent to their needs and their poverty, God will also be indifferent to his needs and poverty.(39)

> The dependents whom a man leaves behind him are our responsibility.(40)

> The ruler is the supporter of him who has no supporter.(41)

Similar evidence is provided by the precedent of caliph Umar, who is reported to have met an elderly Jew begging in the market place of Medina. After enquiring into the man's condition, the caliph assigned him an allowance from the public treasury. It was unfair, the caliph remarked in explaining his action, that the man had paid the *jizyah* (a tax or levy paid by non-Muslims in lieu of military service) while he was able but should be a left destitute and neglected in his old age.(42)

The caliph Umar obviously saw it as his duty to attain distributive justice in the community. He affirmed this when he said, in a public address, that everyone had an equal right in the wealth of the community; that none, not even himself, enjoyed a greater right to it than anyone else; and that if he were to live long enough, he would see to it that even a shepherd on Mount Sinai received his share from the public wealth.(43) Caliph Ali was likewise merely reiterating the *Qur'an* when he stated that "God has made it obligatory on the rich to provide the poor with what is adequate for them"(44) (cf. *al-Dhariyat* 51: 19).

Islam's emphasis on distributive justice found vivid expression in the view advocated by Abu Dharr al-Ghaffari, a prominent companion, who maintained that Islam did not permit a Muslim to accumulate wealth beyond his needs, and that surplus wealth should be expended on community welfare and assisting the poor. This was, however, an unusually outspoken view; for despite their consensus on the welfare obligation of the state, Muslim jurists have also held that acquisition of wealth through lawful means is not against the teachings of Islam.(45)

Administrative centralism

Authority in the Islamic state is vested in the office of the *imam*. He is the central figure in the state who is entrusted by the community with general authority (*wilayah*) by virtue of the contract of representation (*wakalah*) made through his election. The *imam* then delegates his power to other officers of state, ministers, governors and judges, all of whom represent him in their various capacities.(46)

With the exception of judges whose position in enforcing the *shari'a* was parallel to that of the *imam* himself, all other officials acted, in effect, by exercising a delegated authority as assistants to the head of state.(47) Both political authority and administrative power in the state were modeled after the pattern that operated during the lifetime of the Prophet and the period of the *khulafa rashidun*. They all exercised their authority directly or delegated it to others at their discretion and convenience. The officials concerned exercised their delegated authority in their capacity either as leading executive officers of state who partook in *hukm*, that is political authority, or in their capacity as assistants. The leading executive officers were in turn assisted by deputies and assistants who acted as administrative officers but who did not partake in *hukm*. The prerogative of unrestricted political and executive authority thus belonged exclusively to the *imam*, who was vested with it by virtue of the community's pledge of allegiance (*bay'ah*). This theory of government did not recognise autonomous individuals and organs requiring no authorisation from the head of state.[(48)]

It remains to be added that the centralised pattern of administration is founded primarily upon custom, which was in turn reflected in the writings of jurists on the subject of *khalifah*. But there is nothing in the *shari'a* sources which imposes any mandate or restriction concerning the administrative pattern of the state. The matter thus remains open to considerations of public interest (*maslahah*). The head of state is required as the *Qur'an* provides (*al-Imran* 3: 159; *al-Shura* 42: 38) to conduct the affairs of state through consultation (*shura*) with the community. It is through this method that necessary adaptation and adjustment in the administrative structure of the state may be implemented.

Limited government

Islam advocates only a limited government whose power is restricted in a variety of ways. With reference to sovereignty, we note that the Islamic state is not a sovereign state in the strict sense of the word; its powers regarding legislation are limited by the terms of the *shari'a*. Politically, this rules out all forms of absolutism; legally, it paves the way for development of constitutional norms and standards by which to limit state powers. The Islamic state is a consultative state. It is bound, as already noted, by the requirement of consultation and must have due regard for the wishes of the community. The powers of the head of state are also limited by reference to *khilafah*, which means that he acts in the capacity of a trustee: of both Allah s.w.t. and of the community of which he is an employee and representative. The community is entitled to depose the head of state in the event of a serious breach of trust, flagrant deviation from *shari'a*, or loss of capacity to discharge his duties. Furthermore, the individual in an Islamic state enjoys considerable autonomy, since many aspects of his life in the community remain outside the domain of law and government.[(49)]

The jurists have thus drawn a distinction between religious and juridical obligations. Only the latter are enforceable through formal objective sanctions, but most of the religious aspects of the individual's life in society are private and non-justiciable. Even some of the religious duties such as *salah*, fasting, the pilgrimage (*haj*) and much of what is classified as recommendable (*mandub*) and reprehensible (*makruh*) are not legally enforceable.

Government, moreover, has no authority to waive or to grant discretionary changes in the private rights of the individual, which are generally known as *haqq al-abd*. The head of state and judges do, on the other hand, enjoy limited powers to grant a pardon or require repentance in certain cases, as well as to order discretionary punishments for violations of public rights (*haqq Allah*).

Government officials, we may further note, including the head of state, are subject to the rule of law in precisely the same way as are other members of the community. They are accountable for their conduct and enjoy no special immunity or privilege before any court of justice.[(50)] The *shari'a* provides for no special tribunals or jurisdictions for government officials, nor indeed for any group or class of individuals.

Finally in this regard, the *shari'a* limits the authority of government regarding taxation in at least five ways: (1) tax must be just and proportionate to the ability of the taxpayer; (2) it must apply to all without discrimination or favour; (3) taxation must aim at the minimum of what is deemed necessary; (4) the well-being of the taxpayer must be observed in determining the quantity and method of collection; and (5) taxation must observe the time limit of one calendar year for the yield upon which tax may be levied to materialise.[(51)] Abu Yusuf and al-Mawardi both emphasised fiscal moderation by insisting that taxation must in no case deprive the taxpayer of the necessities of life.[(52)]

Government by representation

An Islamic state is not, strictly speaking, a form of direct government of the people by the people. It is a government of the *shari'a*. But in a substantial sense, it is a popular government since the *shari'a* validates the will and endorses consensus of the people.(53) The head of state is elected by the community through consultation, nomination, and *bay'ah* (pledge of allegiance). *Bay'ah* is, to all intents and purposes, equivalent to a vote. Hereditary succession, which was developed under the Umayyads, is anomalous and contrary to the precedent of the *khulafa rashidun*.

The head of state is only one among an entire community of equals, and he rules by virtue of the trust which the community has reposed in him. This popular vicegerency, which forms the basis of democracy in an Islamic state, means that government can be formed only with the consent of the people and that it may remain in office only so long as it continues to enjoy their confidence.(54)

The Islamic state has features in common with democracy and is, in many ways, committed to the democratic ideals of justice, equality and basic liberties. The separation of powers, which is a pillar of western democracy, is also upheld in the Islamic state. Legislative authority through the modality of *ijma* is a prerogative of the *umma*, not of the state. The head of state must implement the rulings of *ijma*, and is himself bound by it.(55) The state is also under a duty to conduct its affairs through consultation with the community. The decisions of the consultative assembly of the state are, according to one view, binding on the head of state and recommendable (*mandub*) for implementation according to another.(56)

The judiciary is also independent in the sense that it does not adjudicate in accordance with the wishes or dictates of the head of state but in accordance with the *shari'a*. Here the head of state and the judge are both under the same duty, and the judge needs no authorisation from any superior authority in the implementation of *shari'a*. The office of the head of state is basically executive in character, designed to regulate and to administer rather than legislate and originate.(57)

The main difference between the Islamic state and democracy lies in the ultimate or sovereign authority which, under democracy, inheres in the will of the people. This is not so in Islam where the basic structure of values is determined by divine revelation. But within that framework, the community is the locus of all authority. It is the *umma*, as previously noted, whose authority the government represents. The government is accountable to it and the *umma* is entitled to depose a leader who is in serious violation of the terms of his office.

Despite allegations that Islam does not recognise majority rule as it is recognised in the West, there is evidence to show the weakness of such a claim. Majority decision or ruling, often refered to as *jumhur*, enjoys uncontested recognition in the works of Muslim jurists, who often refer to the rules of *fiqh* as being the ruling of the *jumhur*. We may also note here al-Mawardi's illustration of the application of majority rule in the selection of the *imam* in *salah*, where he states: "It is the right of the congregation (*ahl al-masjid*) to elect the *imam*. But if they disagree among themselves, the majority choice prevails."(58) Consensus of opinion (*ijma*) is normally concluded by unanimous agreement of the community, or the scholars and *ulama* who act in their capacity as representatives of the *umma*; but in the absence of unanimity, a majority decision or ruling still constitutes a proof (*wa al-kathrah hujjah*) next to *ijma*. It is even suggested by leading scholars that most of what we know as *ijma* consists in fact of majority opinion.

Furthermore, the *sunna* of the Prophet is replete with emphasis on adherence to the *jama'ah* (lit., "multitude" or "majority"), which is another word for majority rule. Although the people are entitled to exercise their personal liberties, the *sunna* takes a very serious stance towards disloyalty and dissension against the *jama'ah*.(59) This outlook is reflected in the juristic views of the *fuqaha*, the legal maxims of *fiqh* (*qawai'd kulliyyah al-fiqhiyyah*) and in legal doctrines such as *maslahah* (consideration of public interest)(60) and *siyasah sher'iyyah*,(61) whose clear orientation in towards the benefit and interest of the majority. The *shari'a* as a whole, as well as the *juris corpus* of *fiqh*, may rightly be characterised as pro-majority, pro-*umma* and pro-*jama'ah*. The government and *ulama* are under a duty to act in pursuit of the public interest. In the event of a conflict arising between private and public interests, the latter must prevail. Finally, the constitutional theory of *khilafah* is clear on the point that the head of state is elected on the basis of majority vote. Where more than one candidate for leadership emerges, the candidate who has been given *bay'ah* by the majority becomes the *imam*.(62)

Theocracy or nomocracy?

Some observers have commented that the Islamic state is a theocracy. The evidence we have reviewed, however, suggests that Islam does not advocate theocracy. If theocracy is understood to mean government by religious leaders who command holiness and spiritual authority (such as that of the Pope in the middle ages), this is definitely not the case in Islam. In a theocracy the leaders claim to represent God's authority and will, including the exercise of such powers as the pardoning of sins.

Islam does not propose such a government, nor does it vest any particular group of people, be it the *ulama* or religious leaders, with any monopoly over power. An Islamic government acquires its authority from the people and is bound by their mandate.(63) The head of state, in his capacity as representative (*wakil*) of the community, is elected through popular vote or general *bay'ah*. He represents and exercises the authority of the people and has no special claim to holiness. The *umma* is also entitled to depose the head of state when circumstances so require. When it does, the government is bound by the general consensus, or *ijma* of the community.

The claim that Islam is a theocracy is substantially unjustified. It would be more accurate to say that Islamic government is a government of the people (*hukumah sha'biyyah*), with the proviso that the popular will must not conflict with the basic principles of divine revelation.(64) For Syed Qutb the basic requirement of the Islamicity of a state is its commitment to enforce the *shari'a*. By contrast, the form that the state might take, whether or not it calls itself an Islamic state and whether it is led by religious leaders (*ulama*) are all immaterial.(65) Accordingly, the Islamic state may be best and rightly characterised as a nomocracy (rule under the supremacy of law), in which it is the *shari'a* which is supreme—with the proviso, perhaps, as al-Ris points out, that the *shari'a* is not exclusively textual in its determination or form. The *shari'a* permits new legislation through *ijtihad*. The *nusus* of *shari'a* are limited and do not provide for all eventualities. Rather, the *shari'a* contains, as noted earlier, general guidelines which are capable of adaptability and allow for change.(66)

To identify ultimate sovereignty in Allah or to recognise Him as the origin and source of vicegerency (*khilafah*) does not necessarily entail the conclusion that Islam proposes a theocratic government or any clerical dominance within it. Islam recognises no church or clerical order of the kind that is found in other major religions. Islamic political leadership is civilian in all of its attributes. The state is undoubtedly required to observe and protect the values and principles of Islam. Yet a state may be committed to these objectives and values without necessarily becoming a theocracy.

Al-Turabi is representative of the preveiling view among Muslim scholars when he writes, "It should be clearly understood that an Islamic state is not a theocracy".[67]

An Islamic state, Turabi adds, is not a government of the *ulama*, nor is it a government by men alone. Women played a prominent role in public life during the Prophetic era and took part in the election of the third caliph, Othman. Only after that period were women denied their rightful place in public life, but here history was departing from normative principle.[68]

Conclusion

There seems to be general agreement that the Islamic character of a state is to be judged by its commitment to the enforcement of the *shari'a*. Often the words *fiqh* and *shari'a* are used interchangeably, but the two differ in that *fiqh* consists largely of juristic opinion and *ijtihad* and therefore does not command the same authority as the *shari'a*. The *shari'a* is not altogether a static set of commands and prohibitions, but consists of principles and doctrines which are dynamic, broad and comprehensive.

The *Qur'an* is emphatic, for example, on the implementation of justice, both retributive and distributive, but it does not specify the details, manner and procedures by which justice is to be achieved. The *Qur'an* and *sunna* also emphasise alleviation of hardship to the people (*raf'al-haraj*) as one of the basic objectives of legislation (*tashri'*). Other major themes and principles of *shari'a* include commitment to the *masalih*, or benefits, of the people. The jurists have specified under five headings the broad outlines and scope of *masalih*: life, faith, intellect, property and lineage. All measures—whether legislative, judicial or executive—that are aimed at the protection and advancement of these values are an extension of the *shari'a* and therefore partake in its principles and objectives.

The *sunna* of the Prophet validates *ijtihad* which is designed to both extend the rules, philosophy and objectives of *shari'a* to their logical conclusions and thereby also to facilitate a closer rapport between law and social reality. A broad, comprehensive and correct understanding of the *shari'a* must always favour justice, compassion, and a sound and robust commitment to truth, to equality, to tolerance and to the realisation of the legitimate interests of the people. Any state that is committed to these values and to the basic rights of the people, which facilitates an effective consultative machinery ensuring their full participation and *shura*, and which is committed to protecting the faith and dogma of Islam against heresy, corruption and wrong guidance is of necessity and by definition Islamic, regardless of the name by which it is known or the form in which it may operate.

Endnotes

1. For a more detailed discussion of the characteristic features of an Islamic state, see my recent essay on the subject: Mohammad Hashim Kamali, "The Limits of Power in an Islamic State", *Islamic Studies*, 28 (1989): 323-53. The treatment here of the themes addressed in that published account will accordingly be brief.
2. Cf. *Qur'an, al-Imran* 3: 110; *al-Anbiya'* 21: 92; *al-Mu'minun* 22: 52.
3. Cf. Abdo A. Elkholy, "The Concept of Community in Islam" in Khurshid Ahmad (ed.), *Islamic Perspectives*. London: The Islamic Foundation, 1979, pp. 175ff.
4. Ibid., p. 172.
5. *Hadith* from the farewell speech reported by Bukhari and others.
6. Cf. Jamal al-Din 'Atiyah, *Al-Nazariyyah al-'Ammah li al-Shari'ah al-Islamiyyah*. N.p.: 1407/1988, p. 266.
7. Cf. Ahmad, n. 13 at p. 47; Samir 'Aliyah, *Nazariyyah al-Dawlah wa Adabuha fi al-Islam*. Beirut: Al-Mu'assasah al-Jami'iyyah 1408/1988, p. 27.
8. Cf. Ayubi, n. 21 at p. 7.
9. Turabi n. 49 at p. 243; al-Ris, n. 55 at p. 216.
10. 'Atiyah, n. 6, at p. 35.
11. Abu al-Hasan al-Mawardi, *Kitab al-Ahkam al-Sultaniyyah*. Cairo: Matba'ah al-Sa'adah, 1327/1959.
12. Cf. 'Atiyah, n. 6 at p. 71.
13. Cf. Manzuruddin Ahmad, *Al-Nazariyyat al-Siyasiyyah al-Islamiyyah fi al-Asr al-Hadith*, trans. 'Abd. al-Jawad Khalaf. Karachi: Saad Publications, 1409/1988, p. 29; Atiyah, n. 6 at p. 274.
14. Cf. Atiyah, n. 6 at p. 275.
15. Cf. Muhammad Asad, *The Principles of State and Government in Islam*. Berkeley: University of California Press, 1961, p. 13; Abu A'la Maududi, *The Islamic Law and Constitution*, 5th ed. Lahore: Islamic Publications, 1975, p. 69.

16. Ibid., p. 14.
17. Cf. Abd. al-Ghani Busyuni 'Abd Allah, *Nazariyyah al-Dawlah fi al-Islam*. Beirut: al-Dar al-Jami'iyyah, 1986, p. 28.
18. Muhammad Yusuf Musa, *Al-Madkhal li-Darasah al-Fiqh al-Islami*, 2nd. ed. Cairo: Dar al-Fikr al-'Arabi, 1961, pp. 229ff.
19. Cf. Atiyah, n. 6 at p. 15; Hilmy; n. 22 at p. 122.
20. Cf. Ahmad, n. 13 at p. 145.
21. Cf. Al-Mawardi, n. 11; Nazih Ayubi, *Political Islam: Religion and Politics in the Arab World*. London: Routledge, 1991, p. 15.
22. Mahmud Hilmy, *Nizam al-Hukm al-Islami*, 6th ed. Cairo: no publisher, 1401/1981, pp. 60-61; 'Atiyah, n. 6 at p. 34.
23. Asad, n. 15 at p. 22.
24. Cf. Muhammad Selim el-'Awwa, *Fi al-Nizam al-Siyasi al-Islami*, 6th ed. Cairo[?]: Al-Maklabah al-Misri al-Hadith, 1983, p. 126.
25. Cf. Hilmy, n. 22 at p. 123.
26. Ibid., p. 124.
27. Muhammad Rashid Rida, *Fatawa Imam Muhammad Rashid Rida*, comp. Salah al-Din Munahhid & Yusuf Khuri. Beirut: Dar al-Kitab al-Jadid, 1390/1970, pp. 805-808.
28. Hilmy, n. 22 at p. 123.
29. Thus we read in the *Qur'an* to the effect: "O mankind! We created you from a male and a female and made you into nations and tribes so that you may know one another (not that you may despise each other). Truly the most honoured of you in the sight of God is the most righteous of you". (*al-Hujurat* 49: 13).
30. Kanz al-Ummal, vol. II, p. 154.
31. Abu Dawud, n. 39.
32. Ibn Jarir al-Tabari, *Tarikh al-Rusul wa al-Muluk*, ed. M. Abu al-Fadl Ibrahim, 2nd ed. Cairo: Dar al-Ma'rifah 1387/1967, vol. III, pp. 189-90.
33. Cf. Sa'di Abu Habib, *Darasah fi Minhaj al-Islam al-Siyasi*. Beirut; Mu'assasah al-Risalah, 1406/1985, p. 89.
34. Al-Tabari, vol. III, p. 584. n. 32.
35. Shihab al-Din Ibn Hajar al-'Asqalani, *Fath al-Bari bi Sharh al-Bukhari*. Cairo: Al-Babi al-Halaby, 1378/1959, vol. VII. p. 27.
36. Abd. 'Ubayd al-Qasim b. Sallam, *Al-Amwal*, ed. Muhammad Khalil Haras. Cairo: Maktabah al-Kulliyyat al-Azhariyyah, 1389/1969, II. 234.
37. *Al-Tawbah* 9: 60.
38. Ahmad Ibn Hanbal, *Al-Musnad*, ed. Ahmad Muhammad

Shakir. Cairo: Dar al-Ma'arif, 1386/1948, vol. II, p. 33, *hadith* n. 596.

39. Abu Dawud al-Sijistani, *Sunan Abu Dawud*. Cairo: Isa al-Babi al-Halaby, 1959, vol. II, p. 122.
40. Ibid., p. 124.
41. Ibid., vol. I, p. 481.
42. In oral tradition and textual sources.
43. Muhammad Husayn Haykal, *Al-Faruq 'Umar*. Cairo: Maktabah al-Nahdah al-Misriyyah, 1964, vol. II, p. 233.
44. Abu 'Ubayd, n. 36
45. For further detail see Umar Chapra, "Islamic Welfare State and its Role in the Economy" in Khurshid Ahmad (ed.), *Islamic Perspectives*. London: The Islamic Foundation, 1979, pp. 209ff.
46. Abu Habib, n. 33 at p. 72.
47. For information on the status of judiciary see my article "Appellate Review and Judicial Independence in Islamic Law", *Islamic Studies* 29 (1990): 215-50.
48. Cf. Taqi al-Din al-Nabhani, *Muqaddimah al-Dustur*. Kuwait: no publisher, 1964, pp. 89-90.
49. Cf. Hasan Turabi, "The Islamic State" in J. Esposito (ed.), *Voices of Resurgent Islam*. New York: O.U.P., 1983, pp. 242ff.
50. For details see M.H. Kamali, n. 1 at pp. 345 ff.
51. Cf 'Abd. al-Wahhab Khallaf, *Al-Siyasah al-Shar'iyyah*, 2nd ed. Beirut: Mu'assasah al-Risalah, 1404/1904 & 1984, pp. 59 ff; Umar Chapra, *The Economic System of Islam*. Karachi: University of Karachi Press, 1971, p. 63.
52. Abu Yusuf Ya'qub b. Ibrahim, *Kitab al-Kharaj*, 2nd ed. Cairo: al-Matba'ah al-Salafiyyah, 1352, p. 152; al-Mawardi, n. 11 at p. 194.
53. Turabi, n. 49 at p. 244.
54. Cf. Fathi Uthman, *Al-Fikr al-Qanuni al-Islami*. Cairo: Matba'ah Mukhaymar, n.d., p. 119.
55. Cf. Diya al-Din al-Ris, *Al-Nazariyyat al-Siyasiyyah al-Islamiyyah*, 6th ed. Cairo: Matba'ah Dar al-Turath, n. d., p. 380.
56. Mahmud Abd. al-Majid al-Khalidi, *Quwa'id Nizam al-Hukm fi al-Islam*. Kuwait: Dar al-Buhuth al-'Ilmiyyah, 1980, pp. 149ff.
57. Al-Ris, n. 55 at p. 380.
58. Al-Mawardi, n. 11 at p. 98.
59. Al-Ris, n. 55 at p. 360.
60. For details see M.H. Kamali, "Have We Neglected the *Shari'ah* Law Doctrine of *Maslahah?*", *Islamic Studies* 27 (1988): 287-304.

61. For details see my article "*Siyasah Shar'iyyah* or the Policies of Islamic Government", *The American Journal of Islamic Social Sciences* 6 (1989): 59-81.
62. Al-Ris, n. 55 at p. 368.
63. Sayyid Qutb, *Al-'Adalah al-Ijtima'i fi al-Islam*, 2nd ed. Cairo: 'Isa al-Baby al-Halaby, 1373/1954, p. 98.
64. Uthman, n. 54 at p. 119.
65. Qutb, n. 63 at p. 98.
66. Al-Ris, n. 55 at p. 377.
67. Turabi, n. 49 at p. 243.
68. Ibid.

Part III:

Umma and Citizenry in Modern Muslim Society

7

Umma and Citizenry in a Contemporary Muslim Country

*Abdullahi Ahmed An-Na'im**

As a lawyer, I would like to address the institutional and structural aspects of this issue. The underlying concern of my analysis is whether there is a tension between "*umma*" and "citizenry" and whether this tension (if any) can be resolved. Do "*umma*" and "citizenry" signify one and the same thing, or are they different? If they are not the same, then what are the implications of the difference between them in a contemporary Muslim country?

Islam: Unity and diversity, plurality and universalism

Let us begin by clarifying what I mean by a "contemporary Muslim country". We have available to us a wide variety of experiences, from North and West Africa to Indonesia and Malaysia in Southeast Asia. There are ethnic, demographic, political and historical differences and complexities involved. We may therefore speak (as many leading scholars do) of there being not only one Islam, doctrinally, but also in a sense many Islams, historically and

* This presentation by Dr. Abdullahi An-Na'im was the first of three major presentations in the symposium session on "*Umma* and Citizenry in Modern Muslim Society".

culturally. By that plural expression I mean the different ways in which Islam is understood in different places, and the varying cultural character and institutional forms that over time it has come to take in them. The various Islams, then, of these countries are not identical, nor are their peoples Muslims all in the same way. While there are universals in being a Muslim, there are also specificities—to be a Muslim at all one must be a Muslim of some particular time and place—and these specificities are not denied or suppressed but acknowledged and accommodated by Islam itself.

But this diversity is neither absolute or chaotic. Despite the diversity in its political, economic and cultural settings, Islam's diversity is bridged and encompassed by a number of universals. The very first of the universals in this diversity is the reality of pluralism itself. What links, across a far-flung world, the unity of Islam's faith and the universality of its aspirations is the fact, and Islam's acceptance, of the pluralism of its adherents. This poses the question, how does the *shari'a* model or an alternative Islamic model respond to this pluralism in relation to membership of the *umma* or to the concept of citizenry?

The second universal factor is the colonial experience. This experience stretches from Morocco to Malaysia. Even if some countries have not been formally colonised, some parts of those countries have had experiences of being protectorates. Experience of the interaction in different Muslim countries between the colonials and the locals has also been diverse.

The third universal is the reality of the so-called "nation-state". The world is now organised as a system of nation-states. Both the component elements of "nation" and "state" and as well as the combined term "nation-state" can be broken down further. For our purposes, I prefer to consider it in the legal sense. Legally speaking, world relations—economic, political or those involving security considerations—are interdependent. One cannot now conceive of a national or international system without the premise of a nation-state.

In all our various experiences or historical existence, our selfhood or identity, both religious and political, has not been defined for or imposed upon us by colonialism because we, as peoples, precede our colonial experiences. We had our own precolonial political, social and cultural systems. Our historical experience has three phases, namely:

- the precolonial experience;
- the colonial intrusion; and
- the reconstituted self in the postcolonial system.

In our attempts at reconstituting ourselves, we often try to reach back to our precolonial existence in the hope of retrieving and reliving some past identity. We have to be careful in this. The colonial intrusion did in fact influence our reality and our self-perception. But it is no longer possible to go back in that way, to relate directly to our precolonial origins. The colonial intrusion ruptured the direct connection, and any possibility which we may now have of retrieving it. Colonial intrusion also transformed the global model into a system of global interdependence.

Islam, the nation-state and global interdependence

What is the constitutional premise of the state in our Muslim countries? Even in Muslim states with no formal constitution like Saudi Arabia, there is still a structural and functional or a virtual constitution: a system of governance and some principles governing the relationship between citizens and the state, among the organs of the state, between those organs and citizens, as well as between citizens themselves.

Each country has as its constituents the population of that country. In many countries which are identified as Islamic countries, the citizenry as constitutionally defined includes all those who permanently reside in that state whether from birth, immigration or marriage, and so on. As a general rule, all those who were permanently residing in that country at the time of independence (and presumably therefore their descendants as well) are citizens. These include both Muslims and non-Muslims. I would like to emphasise here that my use here of the phrase "non-Muslim" is not intended to make an issue of belief or non-belief of that person. Rather, it is used as a reference point in our discourse. It is not religion *per se* that is relevant here but the constitutional recognition and significance that may be given in a modern state to religious difference, especially in connection with definitions of citizenship and of the boundaries of the national community. The attribute or quality of not being a Muslim has its implications for people in terms of their rights as citizens in an Islamic state under *shari'a*.

At the time of our independence, it is important to note, a significant proportion of the population of many Muslim states were non-Muslims, and in many cases that still remains true today. In my country, the Sudan, at least one-third of the poulation are non-Muslims, mainly animists. In *shari'a*, animists are not believers by any definition. Non-believers are non-persons for purposes of statehood under the *shari'a*.

Global society and international human rights instruments

Under currently prevailing *shari'a* definitions, the term "*umma*" in effect means or presumes a "unity in faith". How "faith" is defined must therefore also be considered.

In debating these issues, we must also recognise another dimension—the dimension of international human rights documents. The earliest such document is the Universal Declaration of Human Rights of 1948 which was followed by several major treaties. Although many of our governments have not ratified some of these treaties, most of our constitutions reflect or are inspired by the values that are set out in these documents. Muslim countries which have ratified any of these treaties are bound by it. The Universal Declaration and the other various human rights treaties laid down a very important concept for our purposes: namely, that of "equality before the law". All citizens must be accorded equality before the law without distinction on grounds of religion, gender, race and so forth.

The principle of self-determination of the people is another guiding principle embodied in human rights documents and enshrined in many of our constitutions. How this second principle is to be reconciled with the rights of individuals as individuals, and the question of which particular historical communities and populations are to be recognised as peoples entitled to self-determination, are difficult issues here. But the self-determination of one group cannot be at the expense of another group. You cannot allow self-determination to Muslims and deny it to the non-Muslims of the same country.

Ideally, in any state, the population in its diversity should be linked and merged and meshed together in social interaction. The reality of our plurality and diversity today reflects a history of cross-exchanges and social and economic ties. For centuries, Muslim and non-Muslim communities have been linked together. There has long been and, within the modern nation-state, there should still be harmony and a respect for both communal integrity and for the personal relationships that are formed across religions and ethnic lines.

Pluralism, human rights and shari'a in the nation-state

How do we now accommodate these realities in an Islamic state which is committed to the *shari'a*, whether it be the Sudan, Iran, Algeria or Malaysia?

Under historical formulations of the *shari'a*, people are classified according to their faith. Whether one is a believer or not is determined by the state upon the basis of *shari'a*, and not the individual's own belief. As a Christian or Jew—that is, one of the protected "people of the Book" (a category which, as defined by Abu Yusuf in *Kharaj*, also includes Zoroastrians)—one's religious and therefore also one's civil status are defined by *shari'a*, and not according to the person's own view of the matter. Muslims are full citizens. Believers who are not Muslims are entitled to cultural and social independence, but not allowed political participation in the affairs of the nation-state. They are defended and ruled by the Islamic state, but they have to pay the *jizyah* or tax for the privilege of being defended by Muslims.

As far as non-believers are concerned, the Islamic state may at its discretion accord them the status of *dhimmi*. According to strict *shari'a* rules, they are allowed to live in the state for only a limited period of time.

What are the implications of the *shari'a* in relation to *umma* and citizenry today? If a country is to be transformed into an Islamic state today, then atheists, animists and agnostics cannot be equal citizens within it. In the 1979 Constitution of Iran, Bahais are not recognised as a "protected minority". Although they had been living in Iran as Iranians before this, the national constitution now denies them any protection as a religious minority, let alone as equal citizens in their own country. I have dealt with this issue in my book, *Toward an Islamic Reformation,* (especially on pages 84-86, in the chapter that discusses the reconcilation of *shari'a* and modern constitutionalism). There I propose an alternative Islamic model which provides for complete equality of all citizens as a matter of Islamic law.

Apostasy: A crime of treason punishable by the state?

Here we should address the issue of apostasy. This is a very significant issue in terms of citizenship. Apostasy is not humanly punishable according to the *Qur'an,* which mentions believers who vacillate between belief and unbelief and the punishment that awaits them from God. The warrant or legitimating basis of the death penalty for apostasy is said to be found in the *sunna.* This is a controversial point. There are several *hadith* (reported sayings attributed to the Prophet) that are sometimes said to support punishment for apostasy. There is one report to the effect that "he who changes his religion, have him killed". Another holds that "it is not legitimate to take the life of a human being, save in cases of murder and changing one's religion".

Supporters of punishment for apostasy in present Islamic discourse seek to equate apostasy or *ridda* with treason, and they argue that it should be punished as such. The reasoning here is weak, and the argument one that is typical of a certain kind of self-serving apologetic literature. Historically, apostasy is known on a certain occasion to have been punished as treason in the time of Abu Bakar, the first caliph.

The historical incident here concerns certain Arabs who refused to pay *zakat* (tithe) and declared war against the state. In this context, and with plausible reason, *ridda* was conceived as a political issue amounting to treason, and was not in any way related to the conscience or faith of the individual. But the equation made on that occasion between *ridda* and treason was a specific one that must be understood contextually and historically. It is not a precedent or warrant for any general, categorical assertion that disbelief is tantamount to treason and must be treated as such.

Even if it were, such an equation is no longer tenable in a multi-religious modern nation-state. But, as the historical clarification offered here establishes, there is no convincing basis anyway for the assertion of any such equivalence. The modern state, under modern conditions, accordingly cannot impose any such punishment, nor under a discerning reading of traditional legal precedents is it entitled to do so anyway.

Apostasy is relevant as a factor in defining "*umma*". Bahais in Iran and other countries and the Ahmadiyyahs in Pakistan are declassified and disqualified as citizens in an Islamic state. Muslims tend to deal with these issues in an emotional and irrational way. A great tension and profoundly un-Islamic attitudes tend to dominate people's behaviour towards the Bahais and Ahmadiyyahs. The faith of these categories is defined by the state, and they are on that basis excluded from citizenship and membership of the *umma*. The Ahmadiyyahs in Pakistan are not allowed to sound the *adhan* (call to prayer) or to identify their places of worship as "mosques".

These are some of the issues which we have to address in our efforts towards realising an alternative to the current *shari'a* model. Here, as a guide to how as Muslims and good faith and judgement we might proceed on these matters, I refer to the reform methodology explained in my book, *Toward an Islamic Reformation*. It offers, I believe, a possible, appropriate and Islamically principled way of resolving these and related issues. It is not possible to explain and substantiate that proposed methodology here. Those who are interested, and the issue is an urgent one for all of us, can consult that book.

I believe that drastic reformulation of *shari'a* is imperative, if we are ever to be able to speak of a modern Islamic nation-state. Whether it be through the methodology I propose or some other technique, Islamic law must provide for the complete equality of Muslim and non-Muslim citizens of any modern nation-state. Other aspects of *shari'a* must also be reformulated to remove discrimination on the grounds, for example, of sex and gender.

Conclusion: Legitimacy and the Islamic state

A modern state may indeed be perceived as "Islamic" by its Muslim citizens. However, the state must also be legitimate from the point of view of non-Muslim citizens as well. In other words, the Islamic legitimacy of the state may be relevant to Muslims without denying non-Muslims their right to have a different standard of legitimacy, be it ideological, religious, ethnic or otherwise. Otherwise, it would be an exclusive theocratic state or sectarian-confessional state, not a modern nation-state at all.

Reference

Abdullahi Ahmed An-Nai'm, *Toward an Islamic Reformation: Civil Liberties, Human Rights, and International Law.* Syracuse, NY: Syracuse U.P., 1990.

8

The Qur'an, Shari'a and the Citizenship Rights of Muslim Women in the Umma

*Amina Wadud-Muhsin**

In his presentation on "*Umma* and Citizenry in a Contemporary Muslim Country", Dr. An-Na'im argued that historical *shari'a* used the concept of *umma* as a community of believers; the later adoption of this position as the basis for defining citizenship in Islamic terms for modern times carries, he suggests, certain awkward consequences for a contemporary Muslim societies and nations.

As defined by historical *shari'a*, the state, he contends, in Islamic legal theory recognises three levels of citizenry: three different classes of citizens distinguished on the basis of belief, as construed in conventional *shari'a* terms. These comprise the Muslim *umma* who as full citizens have exclusive political power; the "people of the book", whose definition has been broadened somewhat in modern Muslim history and who as a second class of citizens (even second-class citizens) merit protection but must must pay for it through special taxation; and the unbelievers who do not merit or have no entitlement to any protection within an Islamic state.

---

* The text published here is a *précis* of the presentation by Dr. Amina Wadud-Muhsin, which was the second major presentation in the symposium session on "*Umma* and Citizenry in Modern Muslim Society".

Muslim women as citizens?

One would have thought that Muslim women would unambiguously have fallen within the first category as they constitute an integral part of the *umma*, and even reproduce it. Yet no such automatic inference follows in orthodox Muslim constitutional thinking. In the Islamic state as imagined in conventional sociopolitical theory, women are second-class citizens enjoying no right to self-determination. In historical *shari'a*, Muslim women are simply appendages to their men, first their fathers and brothers, later their husbands (and possibly, at the end of a long life, finally their sons). Within historical *shari'a*, the situation is one where Muslim men exercise domination over women and enjoy a monopoly of political power and force.

In the historical process of their colonisation, the populations of many of what are today considered Muslim states were pluralised in terms of race and creed. This historical development has now brought out the latent tension that is inherent in a definition of citizenship according to faith. With their diverse populations—including Muslims of different origins and cultural identity as well as diverse types of non-Muslims—various Muslim states are now left to grapple with the postcolonial task of nation-building, on the foundation of the pluralised social order that was left as the legacy of colonialism. Amid this complexity and uncertainty, many Muslims in their confusion have looked to historical *shari'a* for the constitutional basis of some new, encompassing and non-Western polity. But while Islam understood as historical *shari'a* at first beckons brightly in these troubling circumstances, recourse to it as the basis of some new political order only yields greater, even more intractable problems.

Just as Dr. An-Na'im argued earlier that, under these dramatically transformed circumstances of ethnic and religious differentiation, historical *shari'a* is no more tenable, in the same way it cannot now be appropriately implemented because of its inability to accommodate modern understandings of gender relations and the status of women. Because it is male biased, a new interpretation needs to be arrived at—which it readily can—through a new methodology of Qur'anic interpretation. Such a methodology can provide modern Muslims, both men and women, together with their fellow citizens in a pluralistic world with a contemporary and appropriate understanding of *shari'a*, distinct from historical *shari'a*. That new understanding must rest upon, and give expression to, a more egalitarian concept of citizenry that can encompass all—regardless of differences of culture and gender—who are permanent residents within the boundaries of the nation.

New methodologies of Qur'anic interpretation

How such a new methodology of Qur'anic interpretation can be developed and applied I have outlined elsewhere (Amina Wadud-Muhsin 1992). But central to any effective challenge to the conservative character and effects of historical *shari'a* must be a focus on Qur'anic interpretation and the *Qur'an* itself.

Reemphasising the centrality of the *Qur'an* can break the popularly received image of women's role and status in the family. Their contributions, which are fast becoming more complex and which straddle both private and public space, should be given due recognition. A holistic reading of the *Qur'an* will reflect these changes in women's contemporary circumstances and provide women with an enhanced economic status and expanded opportunities for productive, rewarding and challenging economic employment.

Such economic empowerment is fundamentally relevant to the question of women's citizenship within the *umma*. For citizenship is not simply an abstract, constitutional matter but must be made concrete if it is to be effective and meaningful. Economic participation cannot be separated from citizenship, not simply because it can transform women's dependence upon and social subordination to men.

More than that, politicial citizenship remains an empty abstraction if those who on paper enjoy it have no economic autonomy; and the social empowerment that such an active and autonomous economic role may provide can enable women to give meaningful and independent content to the otherwise empty shell of formal citizenship within an Islamic polity.

None of this, it should be finally noted, is really terribly radical. It is all entirely consistent with Qur'anic ethics and imperatives, if we understand the Qur'anic text through appropriately modern methodologies, a modern hermeneutic. Such flexibity in devising new and newly appropriate forms for the realisation of enduring

Qur'anic and *shari'a* principles can even be grounded in unimpeachably orthodox expositions of Islamic jurisprudential thinking, as Dr. Hashim Kamali's presentation showed.

He might not accept all the details that others would like to insist upon; but he is in no doubt, as his presentation argued, that it is for the Muslims of every period to discover the form for the realisation of enduring Islamic principles that is most suitable to their times and needs.

If, as he argues, the legal heritage of Islam is a flexible one with a rich capacity for adaptation, then we should intelligently avail ourselves of those interpretive possibilities—in our own interests and in the interest of Islam itself.

Muslim women, in particular, have the right to avail themselves of those interpretive possibilities to redress the long-standing bias against them which has characterised orthodox Qur'anic interpretation and the conventional understandings of *shari'a* that have been based upon it. New interpretation, especially interpretation by modern Muslim women, can renew the strength and flexibility of Islam by reactivating its adaptive genius. In doing so, Muslim women will not be indulging in heretical innovation but simply recalling the true spirit and message of the *Qur'an*. They will be enlarging the social space within the actual world of contemporary Islam, making it coextensive with the moral breadth and spaciousness of the Qur'anic vision itself.

Reference

Amina Wadud-Muhsin, *Qur'an and Woman*. Kuala Lumpur: Fajar Bakti Sdn. Bhd., 1992.

9

Umma and Citizenry: Civil Society in the New World Order

*Norani Othman**

Instead of speaking of the "Muslim world" we need a debate that refines our perception of the Qur'anic term *umma* and makes it more than an abstraction. *Umma* does not imply merely the community of all those who profess to be Muslims. The single most important implication of *umma* is that it is a moral conception of how Muslims should become a community in relation to each other, other communities and the natural world. It is manifesting in thought, action and openness a distinctive moral vision that is the *raison d'étre* of the *umma*. It is an enduring commitment to the dynamism of a constant set of moral concepts and precepts that creates the contours and ultimate configuration of the *umma* ... The unifying force of the concept of *umma* is important in another respect, that of its underlying cultural precepts. The *umma* is not a cultural entity patterned on the norms of any

* Norani Othman's presentation appears here as a third contribution to the debate on "*Umma* and Citizenry in Modern Muslim Society". The author acknowledges the assistance of Clive Kessler in clarifying the argument and improving its written presentation.

> one dominant group nor is it the product of cultural contingency. It does not embrace cultural relativism but exists within and is expressed through diverse cultural groups. As both concept and practice, the *umma* in history provides a demonstration of diversity within unity. This has enabled the history of the *umma* to be marked by an extremely rich interaction with other intellectual traditions (Anwar Ibrahim 1991: 306).

The position adopted by Anwar Ibrahim in his recent discussion of the concept of *umma* is an appropriate one, which others should now examine and follow through to its logical end and realistic implications. In his argument Anwar Ibrahim properly observes that the reformulation by Muslims today of the concept of *umma* must engage and come to terms with the non-Muslim Other. However, he stops short of providing us with any clear account of how this may be done, what it entails, and also what this may ultimately require of Muslims themselves in their capacity and roles as citizens of a modern nation-state, be it Islamic or secular.

Like Anwar Ibrahim, all who are contemporary Muslims, not just historically but in the character of their thinking, would like to actualise Islam in its liberating and democratic spirit. We would very much like to infuse that spirit as a guiding orientation within the structure of the state and throughout the modern political order generally. But the realisation of that spirit within any modern polity on the basis of current understandings of historical *shari'a* has proved impossible. That failure tells us something. The challenge now facing us, as Abdullahi An-Na'im recognises, is to begin a reformation of the methodology of interpreting *shari'a* so that it may become applicable within contemporary nation-states. Similarly, the ideas contained within historical Islam concerning *umma* and citizenry must also be reviewed and reinterpreted, congruent with the needs and criteria of constitutionalism, human rights, justice and equality which pervade the Qur'anic message.

The argument that Anwar Ibrahim presents in his thoughtful article is consistent with the proposal for reformation and renewal (*islah* and *tajdid*) that Abdullahi An-Na'im, and others with not identical but comparably reasoned views of Islam, have advanced. But the question still remains as to the nature of this *umma* and its citizenry that would enable contemporary Muslims to emulate the Qur'anic spirit and implement enduring and authentic Islamic principles in a modern nation-state. In addition, there remains the further question of how to ensure the continuing growth and development of that enlightened model of *umma* and citizenry in a truly modern Islamic nation-state.

A modern Muslim civil society

Anwar Ibrahim's model of the new *umma* can only exist if there is first an understanding of the notion, and also the will to create and sustain, a civil society in a modern Muslim state. What is meant here by "civil society" is a society in which there is scope and space for honest, reasoned and thoughtful discussion, within an atmosphere of principled openness. In this case, these features must be realised within, and characteristic of, a recognisably Muslim society, one which is not constrained by any authoritarian imposition of uniformity or conformism in the interpretation of civil and public Islamic law. Modern states are complex in structure and their populace, the product of many successive waves of history, is inescapably diverse. Modern states must come to terms with this fact of human pluralism and its implications, and they can only do so by accepting it—head-on and gladly. Muslim states are no exception.

The modern state is faced by but also transcends the plurality or diversity of its citizenry; it accommodates the democratic participation of its citizens regardless of differences of gender or religion, culture or creed. The modern state, with its acceptance of the plurality of its citizenry in civil society, does not confuse unity with uniformity. It finds a basis for unity within diversity itself—including a diversity of opinion. It is acceptance of the inescapable diversity in both identity and opinion of modern people who together share the world, and also some particular politically constituted or territorial part of it, that is the hallmark of what we mean by civil society and modern citizenship. A kind of democratic coexistence which recognises and embraces difference is the basis of this civil society. The way the state maintains its own unity while accepting the diversity of its citizenry is in its acceptance of the essential plurality of civil society.

Civil society, Islamic reform, and the spirit of the laws

The creation of this type of civil society is critical to the project of Islamic reformation and modernity. So long as we still seek to transplant the historical model of the premodern Islamic state in form—without recognising that Islam from its founding experience provides us not with a model of political structure but an imperative social ethic and moral vision—the problems of double-standards and discrimination within the Muslim state will not be resolved to the satisfaction of all constituents of that state.

Muslims today do not need nostalgic and imaginative reinventions of the classical Islamic state—the endless recycling of the same model of the pristine, even mythical, Islamic state that is the principal stock-in-trade of the fundamentalist ideologues. Rather, what we urgently require is a modern Ibn Khaldun or Montesquieu: a thinker who might explicate in modern terms, and appropriate to modern and still emerging circumstances, *l'esprit des lois Islamiques*—the enduring spirit and animating ethos of Muslim law, society and sociability. That would be a proper contribution towards understanding the constitution of a modern Muslim state.

There is, in other words, far more to what we must understand by the "constitution" of such a state—including everything that is suggested within such an expression as "the spirit of the laws"—than is contained in any written constitution or can be implied by a merely formal or legal constitutionalism. Beyond documents and lofty legal principles we must take account of what shapes the understanding and touches the hearts of everyday citizens. The structure of law and the constitution has a cultural content and a moral foundation; and even in modern times Islam, provided we understand its political message historically, can provide that cultural and moral foundation—not only for Muslims themselves but for non-Muslim citizens as well.

It can do so in a way that is not disingenuously self-serving. That is, it can provide such a foundation in a society comprised of both Muslims and non-Muslims, not by presenting as universal to non-Muslims values that are historically particular to Islam, but by providing persuasive Islamic grounds upon which Muslims may accept the cultural and religious pluralism that the presence of non-Muslims in their midst, or under Muslim majority rule, entails.

Islam will only achieve its truly universal aspirations when it becomes genuinely inclusive towards all humans, in their variety and cultural difference, as they actually are. It will only achieve that when, going beyond self-declared assertions of its own universality, its spokesmen and ideologues cease to pronounce upon the acceptability to non-Muslims—before they have freely spoken or been fully consulted—of its own historically specific outlook and orientation or of its own historically specific cultural formulations of general, even universal, human values.

In his book *Toward an Islamic Reformation* (1990, see especially chapter 4) Abdullahi An-Na'im argues clearly and in great detail that an Islamic justification and support for constitutionalism is not only important but relevant to Muslims. Non-Muslims may have their own secular or other justifications for constitutionalism and for accepting the legitimacy of the state and its laws. Yet so long as all are agreed on the principle and on the specific rules of constitutionalism, including complete equality and non-discrimination on grounds of gender or religion, each may have his or her own reasons for coming to that agreement. But such agreement on the binding nature of constitutionalism, and the plurality or diversity of grounds upon which the citizens of a modern state may come to accept its legitimacy, both rest upon underlying values and commitments that no constitution can specify or require. This is, in fact, what is meant by "the spirit of the laws".

Islam, with its recognition that humankind is one but also plural, and plural because Allah wished it so even though we might have been made one and uniform in our ways (*al-Ma'idah* 5: 48), provides precisely the kind of impressively principled grounds upon which Muslims may welcome such a pluralism of commitments towards and within the modern state—or, if they cannot accept it gladly, upon which they can be asked in Muslim conscience to accept it anyway.

If modern constitutionalism is the legal foundation for the implementation of a modern *shari'a*, then a truly open and modern *umma* such as that which Anwar Ibrahim has conceptualised and advocates is only possible if it is grounded upon the institution of a democratic space for civil society to flourish.

References

Anwar Ibrahim, "The *Ummah* and Tomorrow's World", *Futures: The Journal of Forecasting, Planning and Policy* 23, iii (1991): 302-310.

Abdullahi Ahmed An-Na'im, *Toward an Islamic Reformation: Civil Liberties, Human Rights, and International Law.* Syracuse, NY: Syracuse U.P., 1990.

Part IV:

Islamisation of State and Society

10

Islamisation of State and Society

*K. Haridas**

Introduction

Since I am interested in dialogue, in developing a better understanding between people and in dispelling ignorance, a forum like this provides a welcome opportunity. I am interested in your convictions regarding the "Islamisation of state and society". I have been moved by the spirit of fairness, justice and by notions of universal rights and values irrespective of ethnic origin, gender or religion that are contained within Islamic thought. I do not claim to have great scholarship in the study of Islam, only a profound reverence for the subject. I am open to your conviction about Islamisation of state and society and would like to share some of the challenges such a conviction imposes on us all. To be on surer ground I have quoted extensively from Said Ramadan's book *Islamic Law: Its Scope and Equity.*

Islam is a global faith. When asked to define Islam, the Prophet (God's mercy and blessings be upon him) said, "it is to submit your heart to God and to harm no one by word or deed". This is an

* K. Haridas's discussion was offered as the first of four major presentations in the symposium session on "Islamisation of State and Society".

absolute call of faith. Islam is a faith that is embraced by about a billion people. Only 16 percent of these Muslims have Arabic, the language of the *Qur'an*, as their mother tongue.

Today Muslims are ruled by a wide variety of governments ranging from sheikhdoms to republics. In addition to countries where they form a majority, Muslims remain loyal citizens in almost every modern state. It is a profound reality that millions of people pray daily in submission to God, reciting the *al-Fatiha* and thereby asking to be shown the straight way. They are all enjoined together in prayer five times daily, with the Friday prayer exemplifying their community spirit, as they are also linked in the other pillars of their faith: through the contribution of *zakat*, the discipline of fasting and the pilgrimage to Mecca. I stand in respect of all that binds the Muslim community in oneness.

The passing away of the holy Prophet came after the declaration of the *Qur'an* that "this day I have perfected your religion (Islam)" (*al-Mai'idah* 5: 3). This was explicitly emphasised in his last sermon, "O people, bear in mind what I am saying, for I might not see you again. I have left you two things. If you hold fast to them, never will you go astray after me. They are God's book, and his Prophet's *sunna*".

Principles of Islamic law and conscience

Concerning the Islamisation of state and society Said Ramadan in his book *Islamic Law* observes:

> It could be said that Islamic law is not fully practised in any part of the Muslim world, and that the drive to implement it is the principal objective of a widespread movement which aims at totally changing the decadent status of almost all Muslim countries.

Nothing better demonstrates the strong influence of this movement seeking the implementation of Islạmic law than the undeniable fact that it was the major impetus for the creation of three states which are now members of the United Nations: Pakistan, Saudi Arabia and Libya. (Many Muslims and non-Muslims will share reservations about these examples).

Prof. Joseph Schacht in his *Introduction to Islamic Law* remarks that

> Islamic law is the epitome of the Islamic spirit, the most typical manifestation of the Islamic way of life, the kernel of Islam itself. For the majority of Muslims, the law has always been, and still is, of much greater practical importance than the dogma. Even today the law remains a decisive element in the struggle which is being fought in Islam between traditionalism and modernism under the impact of Western ideas.

To Muslims, the *Qur'an* as the word of God is the absolute authority from which spring the very conception of legality and every legal obligation. Said Ramadan admits that the *Qur'an*, being basically a book of religious guidance, is not an easy reference for legal studies. It is more an appeal to faith and the human soul than a classification of legal prescriptions. Such prescriptions are comparatively limited and few. Those concerning family law, they are laid down in 70 injunctions; civil law in another 70; penal law in 30; jurisdiction and procedure in 13; constitutional law in 10; international relations in 25; and economic and financial order in 10. (Such an enumeration can of course only be approximate.)

According to Said Ramadan, a thorough study of the *Qur'an* and the *sunna* would bring out the following characteristics in their philosophy of legislation:

1. They are basically inclined towards establishing general rules without indulging in much detail.

    a) In civil law: the *Qur'an* urges, "O ye who believe! Appropriate not one another's wealth among yourselves in falsehood, except it be as a trade by mutual consent" (*an-Nisa* 4: 29).

    b) In criminal law: the *Qur'an* declares that "every soul is held in pledge for its own deeds" (*al-Muddaththir* 74: 38), and that "each soul earneth only on its own account, nor doth any laden bear another's load" (*Fatir* 35: 18).

These injunctions state a basic principle in criminal law, that of personal responsiblity, which suppresses all vicarious responsibility in the punishment of the guilty.

c) In constitutional law: the *Qur'an* establishes that "those who answer the call of their Lord and establish worship are those whose affairs are decided by counsel among themselves" (*al-Shura* 42: 38).

   This injunction provides that the believers settle their affairs by consultation. This includes the principle of representation in government.

d) In international law: the *Qur'an* declares: "O mankind! We have created you male and female, and have made you nations and tribes that you may know one another (and be good to one another). The noblest of you with God is the best in conduct" (*al-Hujurat* 49: 13).

   This injunction clearly affirms the oneness and moral unity of humankind, from which it follows that international peace will only be achieved when nations come to know one another, treat one another well, rid themselves of all superiority and inferiority complexes, and recall that the best in the eyes of God are those who are best in conduct. These are all principles without which no international law can exist. What is the use of international law if it does not aspire to cultivate harmony among nations?

2. From the very beginning, these precepts were meant to deal directly with actual events. This law was concrete, not hypothetical. That is, presupposition was basically excluded from its philosophy of legislation, in contrast to other codes of law which legislate upon the presumption and calculation of probabilities. This trend in Islamic law is deliberate and not a matter of coincidence. The Prophet Muhammad said:

> God has enjoined certain obligations, so do not abandon them. He has imposed certain limits, so do not transgress them. He has prohibited certain things, so do not fall into them. He has remained silent about many things, out of mercy and deliberateness, as He never forgets, so do not ask me about them.

3. As a rule, everything that is not prohibited is permissible. Islamic law was not meant to paralyse people so that they might only move when explicitly allowed to. On the contrary, humankind is repeatedly called upon by the *Qur'an* to consider the whole universe as a divine grace meant for them and therefore to exhaust all their resources of wisdom and energy to get the best out of it.

4. Even in the area of prohibitions, the *Qur'an* sometimes adopts the method of patience. It does not prohibit an evil immediately and absolutely, but awaits a gradually emerging readiness in society, in the light of reason and its own experience, to implement restraint and prohibition. A good example is the prohibition of intoxicants.

5. All that the *Qur'an* and the *sunna* have prohibited becomes permissible whenever pressing necessity arises. This is reiterated throughout the *Qur'an*. It is a generally an accepted rule (known as *dharura*t or "duress") among jurists that "necessity renders the forbidden permissible".

6. The door is wide-open to the adoption of anything of benefit or utility, of whatever origin, so long as it does not go against the texts of the *Qur'an* and the *sunna*. The Prophet, in a *hadith* which is universally held to be authentic, stated this most significant principle when he remarked that "it is but for the perfecting of morals that I have been sent to you", thereby not only affirming all the virtues that had been practised before him but also including them as an inseparable part of his own mission.

Non-Muslims under Muslim rule: Qur'anic imperatives

The *Qur'an* requires that "if ye (O Muhammad) judge between mankind, judge justly. Lo! Comely is this which God admonisheth you. Lo! God is ever Hearer, Seer" (*an-Nisa* 4: 58). All moral values, such as justice, equality, honest dealing and the like are here held sacred. They are to be practised, irrespective of differences of religion. Their authority is dependent only on their equity, which recognises no barrier between people. In other words, they are the human standards of an honest attachment to religion and to human sociability itself. In consequence, the more truly "Islamic" in their behaviour and attitudes Muslims become, the better is the guarantee to non-Muslims that these moral values will be practised.

Like any other human being, however, a Muslim may fail to live up to those high standards. But he has no right to attribute his deviation to any Islamic principle, Said Ramadan stresses. Nor has he the right to justify that deviation on any political or economic pretext. For, according to the Islamic concept, moral values are absolute and concrete: they are meant to be realised in action and not merely accepted in theory. They are alive only when people live according to them.

Said Ramadan further acknowledges that the *de facto* status of non-Muslim subjects might entail unfair discrimination, as occasionally happened in the course of history. But their *de jure* status is remains upheld in both the *Qur'an* and the *sunna*. It is a status meeting the highest standards of equity and equality. As an absolute moral imperative, it should be made concrete. This *de jure* status is as securely grounded and binding as any Qur'anic or Prophetic text could be. Every struggle to establish it in practice in an Islamic state is accordingly not merely legal and constitutional; it is also religiously enjoined, and therefore mandatory upon the Islamic state itself and its leaders.

Religious conscience is therefore not only not opposed to such struggle, but absolutely demands and supports it. It was in accordance with this principle that Muslim jurists led the Muslim public in a strong protest against the caliph Walid Ibn Yazid when, fearing a Roman attack, he exiled the non-Muslim citizens of Cyprus to Syria. Not until they were brought back to Cyprus was the caliph allowed to rest.

"This is an eternal and universal injunction," Said Ramadan maintains

> and the best advice, therefore, that I can give to you is to remind you of one of the directives of God's Prophet, that he himself will stand up as plaintiff against all such Muslims, who are unkind to those non-Muslims who have entered into an agreement with them, and who tax them beyond endurance.

The *Qur'an* is quite clear that ultimately everybody will have to account for his or her own actions. Nobody shall be held responsible for, or may assume the moral burden of, anybody else's actions. This obligation here is the obligation upon Muslims of ensuring justice to non-Muslims living among them.

Stressing a spirit of humanity, Said Ramadan says that the authority of moral values, in the name of Islam, does not merely transcend every difference of religion. It goes far beyond that. One of Islam's moral principles is the conception that human beings, wherever they live, are fundamentally one and the same. As the *Qur'an* urges, "O men, revere your Lord, Who created you from a single mould and made out of it a pair, and thereupon brought forth multitudes of men and women" (*an-Nisa* 4: 1).

The goal of human life, then, is for people to come closer together and to know each other better, not to become estranged from and hostile to one another. The *Qur'an* declares,

> O people! Behold, We have created you from a male and a female and made out of you nations and tribes so that you may know one another (and be good to one another). The noblest among you before God is the best in conduct. Behold God is the Knower, the Aware (*al-Hujurat* 49: 13).

This, Said Ramadan says, implies that the Muslim, by virtue of his faith, should be deeply attached to humankind as a whole and conscious of the fact that geographical borders, political divisions and differences in appearance, race or language must not become a barrier between people. Or as Canon Taylor put it,

> Islam thrust aside the artificial virtues, the religious frauds and follies, the perverted moral sentiments, and the verbal subtleties of theological disputants, It replaced monkishness by manliness. It gave hope to the slave, brotherhood to mankind, and recognition to the fundamental facts of human nature".

Nation, nationality and Islamic principles

The very term "nationality", which is a derivation from "nation", implies a historic attachment to the distinctions of race, common descent, language, history or political institutions. All have entered into the legal definition of "nationality". That is why many principled thinkers, non-Muslim as well as Muslim, have warned us against confusing nationality, in the sense of ethnic or cultural or racial identity, and nationality as membership or citizenship in a particular nation. There is no such confusion in Islam. Of all this often confusing complex of sometimes conflicting meanings, Islam finds acceptable only the administrative concept of nationality. That concept refers to membership in an administrative or political entity, a membership which in Islam as in the modern world is open on an equal basis to people of differing ethnic identities or cultural background. Such a territorially-based political organization should be so administered that no prejudices and no considerations other than binding ideals and moral values are allowed to divide people, individual from individual or group from group.

"Nationality" should neither involve any separating barriers between human beings nor imply a narrow conception of nationalism based on any alleged supremacy of some people over others on linguistic, cultural or ethnological lines. In other words, the quality of people's membership in a particular nation or state can only be determined on the grounds of each member's basic allegiance to his or her own conscience: a conscience which is free of all prejudices. The political status and allegiance arising from membership in a national political community are to be based upon two fundamentals:

1. allegiance to one's own conscience, and

2. social allegiance to the society in which one lives.

Any deviation from either of these fundamentals constitutes a form of hypocrisy, individual or social, since sound membership of a society can only result from conscientious reciprocity. But once conscience is involved, religion enters with its claim to authority. This has happened throughout history. Whether one likes it or not, conscience and religion are intimately linked; indeed, they are one and the same in every religious conception and in every religion.

How, then, can social life be built up among people whose consciences are governed by different religions? An adequate answer to this question involves, however, ethical reasoning, and is therefore not altogether relevant to this present discussion. But the fundamental requiremnet is clear: that in any society religion should be given its proper place, so that every individual may act in accordance with his or her good conscience. This will enable all individuals to cooperate despite their adherence to different religions, Said Ramadan confirms.

This is particularly true of Islam, which, since its inception, not only discarded all artificial barriers between people—individually and as groups—but further introduced the objective conception of the ethnological oneness of all humankind as a matter of faith and of policy. In Islam, the ethnological plurality and the ontological unity of humankind are two sides of the one coin. Each entails and enriches the other.

Such a reconciliation of plurality and difference did not only occur among Muslims in the Islamic state. Under Islam in the age of historical glory, this same notion had a wider, all-embracing significance. It was actualised not simply among Muslims but also between Muslims and non-Muslims—among people of different religions who lived side by side as equals. In his history of Spain entitled *Histoire d'Espagne*, the Spanish historian Romera Navarro observed that

> under [the Muslim] regime, the Hispano-Roman and Visigothic inhabitants of the peninsula preserved their property, their laws, their judges, their churches and their priests. The living conditions of the cultivators of the soil, of the slaves and of the Jews were much improved. The Jews, in particular, who had been cruelly persecuted during the period of Visigothic monarchy, enjoyed during the Arab epoch entire liberty; they were allowed to participate in the new government and to occupy positions in its administration ... There, men of all sects and of all races lived together in liberty. While in Christian Europe fanaticism reigned, here tolerance was practised.

Arnold Toynbee similarly maintained that

> as things are now, the exponents of racial intolerance are in the ascendant, and if their attitude towards "the race question" prevails, it may eventually provoke a general catastrophe. Yet the forces of racial toleration, which at present seem to be fighting a losing battle in a spiritual struggle of immense importance to mankind, might still regain the upper hand if any strong influence militating against race consciousness that has hitherto been held in reserve were now to be thrown into the scales. It is conceivable that the spirit of Islam might be the timely reinforcement which would decide this issue in favour of tolerance and peace.

Reality and trends

In today's ideological vacuum, can encouraging not simply a grudging tolerance of others but the positive acceptance of human plurality, as part of God's favour and *fitrah* to humankind, be amongst the positive roles of Islam? I am inspired by all that I read and hear, but what is the evidence that reality poses before me? Here I acknowledge that it is unfair to judge a faith by its adherents. The deficiencies in reality, and the ways in which it departs from or falls short of the noble religious ideals and visions that motivate us, do not only arise from insistent socioeconomic and political processes. They also result from the subjugation of people not simply to injustice and oppressive social conditions but to their own weaknesses and moral failings.

In a multiethnic, multireligious society like Malaysia, the more inclusive, universal, overarching views of Islam are often contained and compromised by local issues. The state, the politics of the day, and appeals to religion that are made with whipped-up emotions in the context of adversarial politics all contribute to the presentation of a version or understanding of Islam and of an Islamic reality that are politically expedient.

The forms, the externals, the emphasis, and the exhortations through the media also distort the pristine purity of Islam. Islam is state-led and is often politically manipulated. As a counter-reaction, there develops an outlook or mind-set among non-Muslims that stresses the negative aspects of such initiatives. Materialism seems to be all that transcends this sociocultural and political dichotomy, the only bond that links and sustains sociability between citizens on the two sides of this religious duality.

Malaysian non-Muslims stand by the existing social contract and the constitution. They fear the imposition of the *shari'a*. The grounds for their apprehensions are often evidenced in attitudes towards them and to some extent in the way they are treated. If less than enlightened and principled understandings of Islam are used to justify attitudes towards, or the treatment of, non-Muslims that fall far short of the Qur'anic ideals outlined above in this discussion, how much worse—we are entitled to wonder—may things become once *shari'a* law (or rather a certain limited version or understanding of it) is enforced in this country? Who, we are entitled to ask, will enforce it, in what spirit, and with what breadth or otherwise of understanding of Islam's founding Qur'anic imperatives?

This is, my experience tells me, an anxiety not only among non-Muslims. Many Muslims too, it appears, even if they do not openly and in principle oppose all measures for the implementation of *shari'a* law, are worried: that the manner and spirit of any such implementation with be narrow, restrictive and legalistic, lacking all awareness of or sympathy with the impressive cultural openness, inclusiveness and cosmopolitanism of Islam. Instead, like many non-Muslims, as they look at so much of what has already happened and been justified in recent years under the name of "Islamisation of state and society" in this country, many Muslims also quite noticeably fear that the spirit of any now conceivable process of *shari'a* implementation will be regressive and repressive—contrary to the religiously merciful and socially open and uncoercive character of the spirit of Islam in its founding and professedly authentic form.

If, in the light of these past experiences, Muslim citizens are right to feel and also express profound anxiety about impending developments in the area of *shari'a* enforcement, the nation's non-Muslim citizens are no less entitled to do so, on both constitutional grounds and also out of an understandable apprehension that religious freedom and pluralism and the accommodation of difference are about to be abridged.

It is not Islamisation, as understood in accordance with the highest spirit and ideals of a cosmopolitan Islam, that non-Muslims fear, but the non-progressive nature of much of what has been and is likely yet to be done under the name of Islamisation. Non-Muslims such as myself who, out of genuine human interest and in an attitude of spiritual openness, have sought to inform ourselves better about Islam and the traditions inherited by our Muslim fellow citizens are also apprehensive about the justifications that are offered for this narrowing of the noble spirit of Islam, for the nation's Muslim and non-Muslim citizens alike. Such a narrowing does not seem likely to provide the religious, moral or ethical basis in this country for the kind of process of cultural accommodation and reconciliation that Romera Navarro described for Spain up to the 15th century C.E.

In a multiracial society like ours where ethnicity, religion and politics are intertwined, social reality is complex, especially at the ground level and at the level of people's everyday experience. That reality, people's everyday experience, and their various human and spiritual aspirations cannot be summed up in simplistic conclusions or managed through simplistic legal measures or political approaches.

Non-Muslims, on their side, rarely differentiate Malay ethnic issues from Islamic aspirations. The hidden agendas that they see in Malay Islamic aspirations are often more than what first meets the eye. From the non-Muslim perspective, there is a definite need for education, for understanding and for appreciating the Muslim wish to live within an Islamic tradition. The fundamental question which arises here for us relates primarily to the effect this has on non-Muslims. Many non-Muslims, with reason, fear the streamlining of the civil code in accordance with the *shari'a*. This fear is real. While it touches the concerns of Malaysia's non-Muslim citizens, they are treated here in the context of issues which, for their part and in their way, Muslims must address for themselves.

These revolve around such questions as:

1. The equality of non-Muslims in an Islamic state.

2. Varieties in interpretation of *shari'a* and the power of the *ulama*.

3. Issues relating to the principle of *naskh* or abrogation in the context of Qur'anic principles and interpretation: for example, the principle that "there is no compulsion in religion" (*al-Baqarah* 2: 256).

4. The inability of non-Muslims to give evidence against Muslims in *shari'a* courts.

5. The evidence of two women being equal to that of only one man.

6. Issues relating to conversion and minors.

7. Discrimination in the building of temples, churches, etc.

8. Restrictions upon access to the services of and instruction from foreign priests, religious teachers.

9. Enforced removal of symbols.

10. Restrictions upon religious language and the use of certain religious words and terminology, which limit possibilities of interfaith religious dialogue, imply an inferiority or reduced permissibility of some faiths, and which impose and institutionalise a basic split not only between Muslim and non-Muslim religious discourse but among the citizens of a multiethnic and multireligious nation.

These concerns are widely shared and communicated among non-Muslim Malaysians. At times the way in which they are presented to non-Muslim audiences from pulpits and by priests polarises the issues. The representation and understanding of the *shari'a* is often negative and simplistic (though, in their own way, no more simplistic than certain contrasting understandings of *shari'a* that are prevalent among equally unsophisticated Muslims). Non-Muslims remain largely unware of the holistic, universal, all-embracing spirit of Islam (but they are not themselves alone responsible for this ignorance, to which much of what has been done under the name of "Islamisation" has made its own greatly negative contribution), Regrettably, consultation between Muslim *ulama*, especially those of a more progressive outlook, and non-Muslim religious leaders remains minimal.

Questions remain as to the nature and extent of any envisaged Islamisation of state and society. Would it call for or entail a drastic reappraisal of Malaysian society? To what extent would the universal injunctions explicitly stated in the holy *Qur'an* come to bear within, or be allowed to set limits or impose a veto upon, any such process of Islamisation? Can distinctions based on ethnicity be justified in Islam? If not, is a complete reappraisal of the economic, political and social structures of our society called for? Would any such reappraisal, or a rejection as un-Islamic of the making of distinctions on grounds of ethnicity, call into question the fundamental premises of accepted economic strategies and our national policies such as those implementing so-called "*bumiputera*-ism"?

Issues centering upon citizenship and nationality will have to be redefined in administrative contexts from an Islamic perspective. "Positive discrimination" based on economic justice will have to be re-evaluated. Guarantees will have to be spelt out to non-Muslims assuring them of fair, equal and just treatment. Would these and other such measures constitute part of any principled package under any Islamisation process?

Or does the resurgence of Islamic consciousness simply aim to provide confidence to the Muslims concerning their central position in the state, and is that why it therefore focuses so much on questions of dress, ritual or restrictions upon food? The question remains whether the movement and the questions that largely concern it are more profound than that. If it is, then, many non-Muslims and Muslims as well have missed something, since voices raising those deeper Islamic concerns in our society are rarely heard.

When one hears about the Islamisation of the Malaysian state and society, one therefore asks whether it proceeds through a tinkering process or whether it addresses human issues holistically. The authentic and humane Islamic spirit must be seen to express itself in more than superficial or external cosmetic changes. It must challenge human conscience and activate the inner growth of our transcendent nature and spirit. Unless they are grounded within such a commitment and approach, these various Islamisation initiatives will be unable to withstand the pressures of ethnic exclusivism, bigotry and state control.

To be meaningful across our entire society, Islamisation measures will need to stress both means and ends, regeneration rather than notional conversion. Only by this kind of Islamisation and in this spirit and on that moral foundation can a fair, just and equitable society be envisioned and developed. This process, in turn, will have its own requirements. It will call for the interpretation of the holy *Qur'an* and the *sunna* in a progressive, inclusive and universal manner that meets the needs of today's society. Is this simply utopia or can it be a reality? This is both a personal question and a joint human quest. The challenge is whether there are sufficient people in our society, in all its various components, who are capable of responding to this call, conscious of the adversity and difficulties ahead.

References

Said Ramadan, *Islamic Law: Its Scope and Equity.* Kuala Lumpur: ABIM, 1987.

Schacht, J., *An Introduction to Islamic Law,* 5th print. Oxford: O.U.P., 1979

11

Islamisation of State and Society: A Critical Comment

*Muhammad Syukri Salleh**

This paper examines the relationship between state and society and focuses on two elements, namely substance and structure. To derive an Islamic state, certain changes are required. The question is, what changes: change in substance without change in structure, change in structure without change in substance, or a change in both?

Islamic resurgence

The recent emergence of a growing awareness of Islam in almost all parts of the world is undeniable. It is evident, among its many manifestations, in increasing discussions of Islam, the more serious attempts to realise its doctrines, and in the establishment of many Islamic movements and organisations. These are clear manifestations of that new awareness. A variety of perspectives and methodologies have been used in this new effort at understanding, reviving and practising Islam. But irrespective of the differences among them, the endeavour in which they have

* Dr. Syukri Salleh's discussion was offered as the second of four main presentations in the session on "Islamisation of State and Society".

been applied certainly reflects the emergence of a deep interest in a religion that seems to have been long ignored. The resurgence of Islam has a strength that can be compared with a waterfall: when harnessed, it becomes the source of energy. Houses are lighted for families. Trains and tram cars move, easing communication among people.

This new religious consciousness arose on the basis of a broad consensus about the necessity to Islamise everything that is considered "un-Islamic". The term "Islamisation" is increasingly gaining in popularity, connoting for some a process of "converting" (in Malay, one might perhaps literally use the term *memuallafkan*) all un-Islamic things—including an aspect of life or a system—into a form acceptable to or within Islam. The underlying assumption of this approach is clear: that, as a result of the penetration of Islamic societies by and the imposition within them of exogenous ethnocentric values, existing aspects of life and the social systems through which it is organised are in fact un-Islamic. They must therefore be realigned and transformed in accordance with Qur'anic doctrine and the teachings of the Prophet Muhammad s.a.w.

What is Islamisation?

To me Islamisation means basically reviving an awareness that each human being is a creation of the higher divine power. As such every individual is accountable in all matters to his or her Creator who, as the creator of all that exists, knows what is best for the whole of creation. This awareness that we are subjects of an awesome and divine power does not reduce us to passive and helpless servants of the Creator, nor does it mean that our human mental and intellectual capacities are limited. That awareness does not make us inert or static. Rather it is a dynamic force that provides impetus to daily human life in all things.

Yet the methods of Islamisation differ from one group to another. Some insist upon Islamising the outer form of social relations and human existence but leave their inner substance untouched. What they accomplish may therefore appear Islamic, yet in content and in its core elements it still remains un-Islamic. Others, on the other hand, enthusiastically urge Islamisation of the substance, but without transforming the existing secular framework of our existence. This approach accommodates Islamic elements, but only partially, and then justifies this containment of their full meaning and impact by invoking Qur'anic verses and *hadith*. But all that it accomplishes is accomplished within and limited by the existing and dominant secular structure of social life.

If the substance is to be changed yet the form remains unchanged, does one really have control of the process of changing the substance anyway, and can one determine what part of the substance will be changed? But if the impetus for change remains focused on questions of form, what happens to substance?

Both approaches are partial and limited, and neither can really achieve what it hopes to. In either case, those who pursue Islamic change remain dependent upon and limited by inappropriate methods that are not their own. Muslim intellectuals are still unable to escape from the entanglement of knowledge in structures of power and domination outside the *umma*. They are unable to dissociate their approach and actions from the dominant Western methodologies and paradigms. Although labelled "Islamic", their analyses conducted not simply by using the prevailing or dominant tools of analysis but within the dominant secular perspective where those borrowed tools and methods originate.

An example: The case of economics

In economics, for example, such scholars still advocate ideas, objectives and assumptions and pursue approaches that emerged from within Western economics: either neo-classical theory or the radical derivatively Marxist alternative. What makes their work different is the addition of justifications based uppon reference to the *Qur'an* and *sunna*. Providing justifications of this kind—for work of an entirely conventional nature that is simply dressed in apparently Islamic clothes—is an important ingredient or feature of so-called "Islamic" economics. There are parallel instances in other fields as well.

Their work tells a familiar story, and offers familiar remedies. The main objectives that we still find in them are the need to maximise productivity, to increase income and purchasing power and to maximise consumption. They offer no redefinition of any basic philosophy, concepts and assumptions. Resources are still considered as limited while wants are still assumed as unlimited.

Poverty is seen by contemporary economic theories as undesirable and is therefore to be eliminated. In the so-called "Islamic" version of this same kind of economics, no attempt is made to understand why, for instance, in early Islam, there existed the ahl al-Suffah who chose to live in poverty and were tolerated by the Prophet Muhammad s.a.w. But this is not his policy all the time. There were also other poor individuals who were asked by the Prophet s.a.w. to go and earn a living. There were also the rich like Sayyidina Abdul Rahman bin Auf who wished to be poor but was not allowed to do so by the Prophet s.a.w.. There were also the poor like Shalabal, who wished to be rich, but he too was also not allowed to follow that path by the Prophet s.a.w. A detailed examination of this Islamic history would certainly lead to the formulation of a new concept of poverty from a genuine Islamic perspective.

Pseudo-Islamisation of state and society

A parallel phenomenon seems to dominate activity in the domain of the Islamisation of state and society. Islamisation of the state is normally viewed as entailing simply the changing of constitutions, laws, and in some cases of the structures of power. Islamisation of society usually refers to transformation of culture and in values, but merely at the ceremonial and ritual levels. Sometimes such change—a kind of pseudo-Islamisation—is even used as a device or stratagem to advance the objectives of the existing secular system. The campaign for a "clean, efficient and trustworthy" society in Malaysia is one example. At other times, superficial Islamisation is pursued by the authorities in reaction to the increasing pressure of the Islamic resurgence itself and to the rejuvenation of Islam that is promoted by various Islamic groups as part of their effort to put an end to the secularistic system under which we now live.

So long as it is based upon this understanding and approach, Islamisation means neither a reformation of the existing structure nor a transformation of the individual self into an individual with strong faith (*iman*) and piety (*taqwa*). In other words, the Islamisation of state and society within this definition leaves the existing structure intact, and even maintains and strengthens it. This approach merely accommodates certain Islamic elements in a partial or fragmentary manner, while leaving the members of society perpetually dominated by their un-Islamic attributes (*mazmumah*).

Such a method employs an accommodative, top-down approach that attempts to assimilate Islam, in an apologetic manner, into the existing national structure and system, without necessarily transforming the members of the society into committed and practising Muslim individuals. The proponents of this deceptively superficial kind of Islamisation may on occasion introduce new "Islamic" institutions such as Islamic banks, Islamic insurance, Islamic pawnshops and Islamic universities. But the implementation of these new measures remains within the existing socio-economic and political structure. Or, on the other extreme, the proponents of change may even decide to implement the *hudud* laws, but without first educating the society, let alone reviving Islamic doctrines and encouraging the comprehensive practising of Islamic requirements. As a consequence, instead of protecting an apparently already good society from a few disobedient individuals, the *hudud* laws are inflicted on the members of the public who are yet to be guided about and do not fully understand the Islamic way of life.

Islamisation of a state cannot really be achieved by insisting on the implementation of Islam merely at the institutional and ceremonial level. The result of such an approach can only be an "Islamic" state that still maintains various un-Islamic[(1)] elements within its system. This is all that "pseudo-Islamisation" can ever really achieve. In the same way, when one follows the procedures of so-called Islamic political economy and tries to Islamise a state simply by developing various materialistic tools that are available within its unchanged secular structure, the result would be an "Islamic" state which may be strong materially but whose people would be spiritually weak.

In both cases, the Islamisation of the state and society would certainly not fulfill what in the *Qur'an* Allah s.w.t. intends by an Islamic state: *baldatun tayyibatun warabbun ghafur* ("a territory fair and happy and a Sustainer much forgiving") (*Saba'* 34: 15). Above all, such a pseudo-Islamic state and society will be denied the blessings promised by Allah s.w.t. who says: "if the people of those communities had but attained to faith and been conscious of Us, We would indeed have opened up for them (all kinds of) blessings out of heaven and earth" (*al-A'raaf* 7: 96).

Towards a genuine Islamic transformation

Both these limited perspectives are characterised by a reluctance to accommodate a "total" transformation of form and substance into an Islamic entity. This may be due to the fear of the unknown, as well as to intense doubt concerning the viability and practicality of a totally "new" and untried Islamic system. In Malaysia, for example, the financial institutions of the country have not been totally Islamised (except for Bank Islam). Sharing those doubts, many Muslim financiers and entrepreneurs are unwilling to transfer their assets and cash to the Islamic bank. Yet, as some commentators in the national and regional financial press have pointed out, some other bankers (such as MBf) have proved willing to adopt the Islamic loan and banking system. Many customers of these other banks, both Muslims and people of other faiths, are said to favour the Islamic banking system: because of its practicality and the attractions of its profit-sharing system.

It seems, by contrast, that the Islamisation of state and society must evolve and proceed from below, through a bottom-up approach, simultaneous with Islamisation from above, through a top-down approach. Islamisation must first begin from within the individual self, with the implanting of faith (*iman*) and piety (*taqwa*) that can eliminate evil attributes (*mazmumah*) and in their place allow noble attributes to flourish. This is the essential foundation of an Islamic state and society. From this foundation emerge an Islamic family and later an Islamic society, in time an Islamic state and eventually a strong Islamic *umma*. What emerges through this gradual process will gradually replace the existing system in both form and structure, producing a self-sufficient society beneficial to all mankind.

To quote Ustaz Ashaari Muhammad, the founder-leader of *Darul Arqam*:

> When the Islamic soul is developed through Islamic faith (*iman*) and righteous belief (*aqidah*), physical development will emerge automatically. But if the soul is not Islamised, all the physical development will take place un-Islamically.[(2)]

And again,

> The Islamic faith (*iman*) never permits human beings to stay static. Islam must be realised in the society. The Islamic *umma* must work; work to Islamise all aspects of physical development such as in education, economy, social life, medical care, politics and anything that we need to live on. And Allah s.w.t. will observe and evaluate those works as worship.(3)

This school of thought which infuses human spiritual and ethical values into materialistic progress has not only been argued at the theoretical level. It has also been practised and its outcomes have proved effective.

References

1. Un-Islamic here refers to un-Islamic values. This is not a discussion of Muslims or non-Muslims as human beings.

2. Ustaz Haji Ashaari Muhammad, "Ikutlah Cara Allah Mendidik Manusia" [Follow God's Instruction for Humankind], in Ustaz Tajul Ariffin (ed.), *Pada Hemah dan Pandangan Ustaz Haji Ashaari Muhammad* [Opinions and Views of Ustaz Haji Ashaari Muhammad], Kuala Lumpur, Penerangan Al Arqam, 1986, p. 90. See also Ustaz Haji Ashaari Muhammad et. al., *Kembara Membuktikan Kebenaran Al-Quran* [Explorations in Proving the Truth of the *Qur'an*], Kuala Lumpur, Penerangan Al Arqam, 1987, p. 204.

3. Ustaz Ashaari Muhammad, "Pembangunan Masyarakat Mengikut Kaedah Islam: Pendekatan Darul Arqam" [Social Development Following the Islamic Method: The *Darul Arqam* Approach], a paper presented at the Social Engineering for Rural Development Workshop, Ministry of Land and Regional Development, Kuala Lumpur, 1984.

12

Islamisation of State and Society: Some Further Critical Remarks

*Chandra Muzaffar**

Islamisation is that process by which what are perceived as Islamic laws, values and practices are accorded greater significance in state and society. It is essentially a contemporary phenomenon, associated with the postcolonial era. In the precolonial period, Muslim societies did not pursue any policy of Islamisation as such. There was no need to since state and society, at least in theory, were supposed to be guided by the *Qur'an* and *sunna*. It was largely because of the colonial interlude which changed drastically some of the fundamental characteristics of the Muslim polity that many Muslims today advocate Islamisation.

Islamisation and the state: Two directions

This desire is one of the motivating forces behind Islamisation. It is, to some extent, a sincere attempt to restore pure and pristine Islam. It is a quest for the Islamic ideal. At the same time, Islamisation is also part of the reassertion of an identity—an identity which was, to a lesser or greater degree, suppressed under Western colonial

* Dr. Chandra Muzaffar's analysis in this chapter was offered as the third major presentation in the session on "Islamisation of State and Society".

rule. Accordingly, Islamisation is, in a sense, an endeavour to establish the uniqueness of a civilisation which refuses to accept Western domination and control. Since Western domination is very often reflected in, and perpetuated through, the policies and practices of secular local elites, Islamisation has also become an instrument of protest against the state. More often than not, the state against which the advocates of Islamisation—the Islamic resurgents—are pitted is an oppressive, authoritarian structure. There are times, however, when Islamisation serves a completely different purpose. The state itself uses it to cut the ground from under the feet of its opponents. Through Islamisation, it tries to increase its popularity and enhance its legitimacy. Islamisation is even manipulated to sanction state control of society.

This brief analysis indicates that in many Muslim societies, both the state and society are involved in Islamisation. In Malaysia, the state has chosen to adopt a piecemeal, *ad hoc* approach. Certain Islamic rituals such as the celebration of the Prophet's birthday are encouraged; certain Islamic institutions like the Islamic Bank are established; certain Islamic values including hard work are emphasised. By emphasising values, institutions and rituals which do not threaten its primary interests, the state is in fact responding to what it sees as an Islamic challenge from society, articulated through the opposition. The opposition for its part—especially the Islamic Party of Malaysia (PAS)—views Islam in its totality. It seeks the total, complete Islamisation of state and society according to its view of what Islam is. An Islamic state is its cherished goal.

There are any number of ruling elites in the Muslim world whose approach to Islam is very similar to that of the Malaysian leadership. In Indonesia, Egypt, Jordan, Tunisia and Morocco, among others, the ruling elite resembles Malaysia's. Similarly, the opposition—or a significant segment of the opposition—in all these countries tends towards the PAS ideal of an Islamic state based upon the *Qur'an* and *sunna*.

Islamisation: Positive and negative effects

Islamisation in most societies, whether it is manipulated by the state or inspired by the opposition, has generated both positive and negative consequences. In Malaysia, for instance, Islamisation has brought about some positive changes at the level of private, individual behaviour. There are Muslim grassroots groups, like the *Darul Arqam*, which not only emphasise courtesy and kindness in interpersonal relationships but are also innovative and enterprising, especially in economic matters. Islamised youths appear to have a clearer purpose in life than do some of the aimless adolescents who "*melepak*" (as current usage describes their lack of purpose) and squander time and energy in frivolous pursuits. At the same time, the rise in Islamic awareness, coupled with Muslim reactions to the suppression of Muslim communities in different parts of the world, has made large sections of the Muslim *umma* quite critical of the West. There is less blind adulation of Western culture and lifestyles today than ever before. Indeed, in some circles, the ideology of modernisation and development itself is being subjected to serious scrutiny.

However, Islamisation has also been negative in certain respects. Islamic resurgents, in their pronouncements and even in their actions, often restrict women's public roles. There is very little understanding or recognition of a woman's individuality, of her integrity as a person. By the same token, in the Islamic state which Islamic resurgents have created, or aspire to establish, people of other faiths find that their status is circumscribed in certain ways. In politics and public administration, they are not expected or encouraged to make any real contribution. Even in other areas such as culture and education, their role is limited. Most of all, Islamisation, from what we can see, has resulted in the emergence of an elite with theological credentials, or backed by the theologians (*ulama*), who insist that their interpretation of Islam is the only correct and legitimate one. They do not tolerate any criticism of their rulings on Islam. They behave as if they have a monopoly of the truth. Consequently, they have introduced an extremely authoritarian and dogmatic strain into the religion.

There does not appear, on reflection, a single country anywhere in the world where Islamisation or the Islamic resurgence has brought Muslims closer to the Qur'anic ideal of a just and compassionate society. Even the Islamic Republic of Iran, which in certain spheres of social life is more genuinely Islamic than many other societies, does not seem to be moving in that direction. Islamisation has not succeeded in imprinting upon the Muslim consciousness the crucial importance of eliminating poverty, exploitation, corruption and greed. Neither has it strengthened the Muslim commitment to interethnic harmony or public accountability or social justice. On the whole, Islamisation has been concerned more with the symbols rather than the substance of the religion, with what is peripheral rather than what is fundamental to Islam. It is a superficiality which is reflected in what we might call the "car-sticker" phenomenon. There are Islamic resurgents who display their "commitment" to Islam by sticking on their car windscreens labels proclaiming that "The *Qur'an* is the answer", "Islam is the best" and the like. But observing their road behaviour soon shows that they are no more courteous or considerate than any other driver. Their actual conduct, in other words, is at variance with what Islam expects of a Muslim.

Islamisation without meaningful transformation?

Why has Islamisation failed to transform the *umma,* both at the individual and at the collective level? Part of the explanation is to be found in the character and orientation of dominant Islam at this time. It is an Islam which is conservative, orthodox and doctrinaire. It is afraid of change and transformation. It is an Islam which is more comfortable with established tradition than with new interpretations of social justice and freedom guided by the Qur'anic vision.

There are of course Muslim leaders critical of conservative Islam who would like to develop a different approach to the religion, to enable its liberating message to shine through. But they dare not make any move for fear that they will lose support among the masses. They know that the *ulama* with their conservative, traditionalist views or version of Islam exercise a powerful hold upon the Muslim mind.

There is another problem. Islamisation loses its impact when its advocates compromise with powerful vested interests in society. In Malaysia, the state's Islamisation policy has never questioned those aspects of capitalism or of ethnicity which are contrary to Islamic teachings. In fact, even the PAS government in Kelantan—the credentials of the *ulama* who lead and support it nothwithstanding—has been quite willing to accommodate the extravangances of the local royalty. In the Islamic state of Pakistan, the *shari'a* coexists with the exploitation of the poor by rapacious landlords. Saudi Arabia is an Islamic state which sanctifies the absolute authority of the monarch, however repugnant it may be to the religion.

It is not just the structure of power or the vested interests within a particular society which militate against Islamisation. The international environment itself is hardly conducive to the emergence of a genuinely Islamic society anywhere in the world. How can an Islamic economy succeed within a global economy which emphasises the unlimited acquisition and accumulation of wealth, encourages selfishness and greed, and neglects the basic needs of a huge segment of humanity? How can an authentically Islamic political system survive in the midst of a Machiavellian political culture which glorifies power, whatever the price? How can Islamic culture flourish when crass materialism and a rampant, exaggerated individualism characterise the lifestyle of the influential stratum of society? Indeed, how can an Islamic society, or any society founded upon God-consciousness and guided by universal spiritual and moral values, retain its integrity and identity when civilisation itself seemingly worships only Mammon? How can one create a spiritual and moral order in one small corner of the earth when the very soul of the planet has been captured by the rich and the powerful?

If genuine Islamisation is therefore to succeed even in one particular country, the international environment itself must change. But will it? And how can it possibly change when the dominant forces of secularism and capitalism seem to be so strong?

Islamisation and the global context

There is perhaps a possibility, even a small possibility, that change in the global structure could occur in the long run as a result of the interaction between the West and Islam. This interaction may or may not assume the form of confrontation, which could lead to eventual conflict. Conflict, needless to say, has been a vital factor in social change throughout human history. After all, every major religion, at its birth, had to confront the dominant forces of the day. The ensuing conflict very often led to the growth and expansion of the new emerging religion.

But Islam and the Muslim *umma*, as it is today, are in no position to confront the West. Islam remains too divided politically and economically to offer any real challenge. Besides, the West itself—more precisely its dominant forces—do not see the *umma* as a homogenous entity with a single collective will and voice.

Consequently, Western powers relate to different Muslim societies in different ways depending upon their own national interests at the time.

Nonetheless, there are certain underlying perceptions, certain overaching considerations on both sides, which have created and in a sense perpetuated the gulf between Islam and the West. There are values and worldviews separating the two civilisations which may even lead to some sort of ideational conflict in the future. More important, there are concrete, tangible economic and political interests which divide some of the dominant elements in the West from some of the influential forces in the Muslim world. This could set the stage for a collision of sorts. (Some in the West itself, such as Professor Samuel Huntington in his now notorious article on the subject, not only anticipate such an eventuality but even find it both inevitable and inviting!)

Seven areas of civilisational contest

There are perhaps at least seven areas of potential conflict between the two civilisations.

1. First there is oil, the lifeblood of Western industrial civilisation. Most of the oil that is exported to the West comes from West Asia and other Muslim countries. The West wants to ensure that it has a firm grip upon the oil taps of the world—which means a firm grip upon societies which happen to have Muslim populations. This explains why the U.S.A. and its allies were prepared to go to war to regain control over Kuwait. It is worth noting, in this connection, that another important oil-producing region of the world that is going to be a significant exporter in the near future—Central Asia—is also a Muslim region. The desire of Western oil corporations and political elites to control the production and export of other people's oil has been—and will continue to be—a major source of conflict.

2. It is not just controlling oil, but the pattern of control over oil-exporting states in West Asia in particular which could bring the West and Islam into conflict in the future. In most instances, the U.S.A. attempts to prop up feudal monarchies which have very little popular support. These monarchies in turn, are

unequivocally loyal to the U.S.A. and other Western nations. This has further alienated the already elitist ruling regimes of that region from their people. The oppostion that is growing in some of these monarchies—notably South Arabia—seeks inspiration from the *Qur'an* and the *sunna*. Some of its leading lights have accused their feudal rulers of betraying the cause of Islam.

Islam first emerged as the rallying point of opposition to pro-U.S., pro-Western monarchies in West Asia in the 1979 Iranian Revolution. Indeed, the Iranian Revolution was the signal to the world that Islam had become a powerful political force in the struggle against Western domination and control in the postcolonial period. Since 1979, even in the republics of the Middle East, it is Islamic movements which provide opposition to pro-Western, secular ruling elites in Egypt, Tunisia and Algeria. Let us not forget that an Islamic movement was robbed of electoral victory by a semi-military junta in Algeria in 1992. That Western governments, the Western media and Western academics quietly applauded the brutal suppression of the people's verdict is proof—if proof is needed—not simply of their often opportunistic attitude towards "democracy" but of their antipathy towards Islam.

3. The growing significance of Islam in the opposition to Western dominance of the Middle East manifests itself in yet another issue: the long-standing political conflict over Palestine. Palestinians, Arabs and Muslims as a whole have always seen the destruction of the state of Palestine and the creation of Israel as stark evidence of the power of the West in the Middle East. But it is more than Western power that deprives the Palestinians of their legitimate fight to a homeland. It is the strength that Zionism represents, not just as the official ideology of Israel but as the worldview of international Jewry which is also responsible for the suppression of the Palestinian people. For a lot of Arabs in the Middle East and for many Muslims elsewhere Zionism is the mortal enemy of Islam. As long as Zionism is protected and perpetuated by the centres of power in the West, the Muslim world will continue to view the West with suspicion and distrust. Today, the most concerted, consistent challenge to Zionism is coming from Islamic groups in Palestine and Lebanon.

4. Islam and Muslims, it appears, are also destined to play a major role in the larger conflict between the West and the rest or between the North and the South. It is becoming increasingly clear that with the end of the Cold War, powerful groups in the North will do everything they can to intensify their domination of the South. The North-South dichotomy, simplistically interpreted, could emerge as a division between wealth and poverty, power and powerlessness, white and coloured. Because Muslims constitute the single largest religious community in the South, because Muslims are amongst the poorest and most powerless people on earth, the North-South dichotomy could also assume a religious character. Even as it is, a sizeable segment of the victims of hunger and famine, of external aggression and internal turmoil, in the South happen to be Muslims.

5. It is equally significant that in the North itself—in Western and Eastern Europe, in the United States and even in Russia—Muslim communities today constitute the most significant religious minority. This is especially true of most countries in Western Europe. There is considerable and undeniable uneasiness in the relationship between the majority European communities and these minorities. Europe, on the whole, has been less than tolerant of the Muslims in its midst, as the sufferings of the Muslims of Bosnia-Herzegovina attest. While the reasons behind Europe's and the West's dithering over Bosnia-Herzegovina are complex, the centuries-old Western bias against Islam has irrefutably played a big part. It is conceivable that other more serious conflicts may erupt in the future which could cause even more damage to the fragile ties between the West and Islam.

6. At the root of these fragile ties, as was just now suggested, is a long history of bias and prejudice, even hatred and antagonism towards Islam and Muslims. The Muslim conquest of parts of Europe from the eighth to the eighteenth centuries C.E., the crusades and Western colonialism have all contributed to this state of affairs. If anything, continued Western domination of Muslim societies and specific episodes in recent decades—including the Arab-Israeli wars, the Iranian Revolution and the 1991 Gulf War—have aggravated the situation. Western

antagonism towards Islam—as certain Western thinkers themselves have acknowledged—runs so deep that it is easy to evoke mass feelings of hatred and contempt for any Muslim personality or action. This means that very little effort is required to mobilise Western public opinion over any conflict involving Islam or Muslims.

7. When all is said and done, we have no choice but to admit that Islam, as an ideology and a culture, is very different from secular Western civilisation. With its faith in one God as the basis of the whole of existence, its all-encompassing system of spiritual values and moral precepts, its comprehensive set of laws embracing all aspects of life and living, Islam, it is true, contradicts the basic postulates of the secular civilisation that rose out of the Europe of the Enlightenment. Can we expect civilisations which are so drastically different to coexist happily? Or is a conflict inevitable?

Transforming Islamisation: Two imperatives

Islamic resurgents worldwide hope that in any conflict between Islam and the West, the former will emerge triumphant. Some are absolutely convinced that Islam will emerge victorious. But how can we expect Islam as it is presently understood and practised to provide an alternative to the existing civilisation? How dare we place our hope in the Muslim *umma* and in our present Muslim leaders to usher in a better tomorrow when they are in such a sorry state themselves!

If Islam is to transform the world—to Islamise the globe if you like—it must fulfil two conditions. First, Islam must be able to offer humankind an alternative civilisation which is far more just and far more compassionate than what exists today. After all, when Islam spread rapidly throughout the world in the early centuries, it was because it offered humanity a social order which was more just than anything that then existed. In other words, an Islam which cannot overcome the iniquities and injustices of the present age—whether they are related to the environment or the economy, to ethnic relations or culture— will not be accepted as an alternative civilisation.

Second, Islam will not emerge as an alternative civilisation, or the moral basis for one, so long as its universal message is presented in a sectarian manner. Islam will have to go beyond its present religio-cultural boundaries—not so much geographically as in its own presentation and even understanding of itself. Its values, principles and laws will have to be interpreted and articulated in such a way that human beings everywhere—whether they are Muslims or not in the formal, conventional sense—will be able to identify with them. As Khomeini put it in his last will and testament, "True Islam is not for Iranians or for Muslims but for all oppressed people in the world regardless of nationality and religion". But for that to happen, our attitude to the human being itself must undergo a genuine transformation. The poet-philosopher Muhammad Iqbal was right when he observed decades ago, "As long as we do not demonstrate by *our action* that we believe that the whole world is the family of God, all our beautiful ideals will remain mere dreams".

13

The Sociopolitical Dimensions of Islamisation in Malaysia: A Cultural Accommodation of Social Change?

*Norani Othman**

Introduction

The process of "Islamisation", both generally and in Malaysia specifically, needs to be explored critically as a phenomenon of social change. Islamisation is viewed here as part of a complex of responses by Muslims aimed at accommodating culturally the impact of rapid and often disruptive social change. In particular, it considers change that has taken place in the *dar al-Islam* or "abode of Islam" as part of its encounter in modern times with the West: initially as the Muslim lands fell under colonial domination and, more recently, the changes arising from the interplay between continuing postcolonial economic dependence and the simultaneous political and cultural resistance to that continuing domination.

Islam has frequently served as the vehicle for what French commentators on the Maghrib have termed the "popular classes" in their efforts to express their alienation from leading

* Norani Othman's presentation was offered as the fourth major presentation in the session on "Islamisation of State and Society". The author acknowledges the assistance of Clive Kessler in clarifying the argument and improving its written presentation.

"Westernised" elites in postcolonial situations. This resurgent response marks the great cultural divide between the beneficiaries of Westernising "modernisation", on one side, and the casualties of the changing socioeconomic order over the past century, on the other. Contemporary policies and ideologies relating to Islamisation are invariably articulated within a wide spectrum of political and social trajectories. These responses include nationalist movements, social movements and movements pursuing various kinds of "citizenship politics" aimed at encouraging the growth of Muslim "civil society", various economic and social development programmes, and movements pursuing various projects of state creation and consolidation.

These Islamic movements which we now recognise as movements calling for the Islamisation of all predominantly Muslim states or societies must also be understood in the present context of the international society. The current repoliticisation of Islam which began in the 1970s has seen the emergence into international prominence of Islamic fundamentalists voicing the claim that there is only one all-embracing culture, Islam, that is valid for all times, places and peoples. Yet these countries that call themselves Islamic are culturally diverse and until recently they have all subscribed to their own culturally distinctive variants of Islam.

At present there are more than forty states throughout the world which have a Muslim majority, although that Muslim majority may not necessarily command the political capacity to define statehood. Meanwhile, even where they have been able to create, according to their own particular formulation, an Islamic state based upon some view of *shari'a* requirements such as in Iran, Pakistan and the Sudan, their efforts have created more problems than they have solved. These problems largely attest to the numerous disagreements that have arisen among Muslim jurists over public law issues (see Abdullahi A. An-Na'im 1990; Mayer 1991).

There has also been a noticeable failure on the part of various national Muslim political leaders and many of the *ulama* associated with them. Together, because of their positions in their society, these two important leadership elements have been mainly responsible in determining the nature and approach of these Islamisation policies. Often, particularly as the political leaders have deferred to the *ulama* on what the latter insist are issues involving specialist religious knowledge and basic faith (*aqidah*), the important distinction has been blurred between texts and context.

Whatever the *ulama*'s understanding of and political motivation in these matters may be, that kind of intellectual deference to them has had an important but unfortunate consequence. Many Muslim political leaders, and with them many of their citizen followers of good religious faith, who do not claim the same religious expertise as the *ulama* have allowed themselves to become confused concerning the difference between law and the social context to which it is applied. They have lost the ability to differentiate intellectually or analytically between two quite separate areas or issues: between, on the one hand, the various textual sources of Islamic law which many Islamic activists wish to see applied (and which can only be applied in any case by being first interpreted, in some particular manner that will always remain contestable through the invocation of some alternative and equally plausible interpretation); and, on the other hand, the domain of social performance and legal realisation, in which legal texts—or rather the legal principles which they are understood to contain—are given social embodiment and effect through human choice, discernment and initiative.

As a result of that deference, and that consequent inability among the majority of leading politicians and ordinary citizens to distinguish between the sources of legal principle and the social structural realities into which those principles are injected, old juristic treatises embodying some of the principles of *fiqh* have been promoted in rank to primary-source status and given binding legal force by government legislation. All this is done in the name of the asserted obligation to implement an allegedly eternal, unchanging and mandatory *shari'a*.

Islamisation

To understand recent Islamisation movements, one needs to view them historically within their sociopolitical contexts. All efforts at the Islamisation not simply of individual human conscience but of society, past and present—with the exception of those by the Prophet s.a.w. beginning in Medina—are ultimately endeavours by ordinary or imperfect human beings to actualise their interpretations of religious ideals. For the sociologist of religion, therefore, a critical examination of Islam, as of any other religion, can never be achieved through a purely philological approach and the mere study of written sources or religious texts. Although familiarity with these sources is a necessary prerequisite or part of any such serious sociological study, it cannot be an end in itself.[1]

The twin aspects of Islam—as faith in the heart and as actualised in society through public policy—underlie the attempt of Islamic jurists, especially the Sunni, to consider *din* as a formulation of public policy where religion, state and faith merge in a single form of action (Rafiq Zakaria 1988; Fuad I. Khuri 1990). The emphasis on religion as public policy has led numerous Muslim political groups—including their thinkers, writers and pamphleteers—to claim that Islam is not only a religion but *din wa dawla*, a religion fused with a state order (Bassam Tibi 1991: 123). Orthodox Islamic and especially Sunni religious discourse is therefore not simply religious in nature but also inescapably social and political as well in its implications.

The inherently political nature of Islamic discourse does not only apply to traditional texts and religious communication. The modern movement of Islamic resurgence and repoliticisation makes it imperative for us today to study how the currently prevailing Islamisation discourse defines change for its individual adherents and for society as a whole. We must also analyse how the approach and practice of contemporary Islamisation are mediated through an Arabocentric interpretation of Islam—and how in consequence the ideologues of Islamisation have anachronistically projected the meaning of modern political concepts such as state, sovereignty, legislation, democratic rights, constitutionalism and citizenry onto the past, while simultaneously importing archaic social and political ideas from a largely imagined or idealised Islamic political past into the present.

This idealised Islamic past is perceived and presented as the primordial or paradigmatic form of democratic government of the people: a democratic order which is also, and first, to be regarded as a divine order—and to be restored for precisely that reason. Yet the idealised Islamic political past that is invoked by the ideologues of Islamisation is not a traditionalist view. On the contrary, it is a vision not so much of the past itself but of the future as a restoration of the past. Yet this future that is derived from the "good old" (*salaf*) ways of early times or *salafiyya* is inferred from a past that has been re-imagined and also legitimated through the mediation and meaning of modern political concepts and terms.

The projection of these modern meanings back into Islamic history has a triple effect. It employs modern political idiom to legitimate an idealised view of the past. It uses that view of the past—one which has been covertly or unconsciously fashioned through the use of modern concepts—to argue for the congruence of the past with the present, and that the application of that model of the past to the present and future is therefore both appropriate and even mandatory. And it also serves the purpose of appropriating the terms of modern, especially critical, political thought into the discourse of Islamisation, thereby making them appear and become culturally understood as authentically Islamic. In this way, modern thought is not only claimed by but also subordinated to the cause of Islamic activism: because in the process, the differences between the modern and resurgent Islamist understandings of these terms are "filtered out", dismissed or minimised and the critical edge of those modern terms thereby blunted.

Any vision of the future that is produced in this way must be fraught with tension between the model and reality. But we must understand how the desire to produce inherently contradictory or ambiguous social blueprints of this kind arises, and what gives them their impetus. The desire to defend and even return to what is seen as tradition, or an idealised past, is always a response to the disjunctions—and a symptom of the disappointments—of incomplete, unsuccessful or obstructed modernisation.

Social change and the Islamic model for reality

The cultural worldview of humans may change side-by-side with changing social structures, but does not necessarily do so. Sociocultural systems can prove resistant to change. For example, Islamic law, the *shari'a,* is regarded by many Muslims as immutable. Law and its role, according to traditional Islamic views, may not change, since the law is said to embody a definitive, final message or truth for the whole of humanity. Its provisions are seen as sacred instructions, entitled to define and structure all aspects of human behaviour.

As an organic religious system, Islam embraces all spheres of life and contains strict commandments of conduct. According to Islamic doctrine, all past, present and future development derives from this divine source, complemented by other historical sources that are said to be authoritative: traditions, originally handed-down orally and only later committed to writing in various discrepant or even conflicting compilations, concerning the Prophet Muhammad's verbal utterances and deeds (*hadith*) which form the practice of the Prophet (*sunna*).

No interpretation of the relationship between Islam and development or social change can avoid an analysis of the historical importance of the *Qur'an*, *sunna*, and *shari'a*. Here again we confront not only the problem of coping with the historicity of early post-Qur'anic Islamic texts but, no less difficult, of how we are to read even the eternal message of the *Qur'an* itself into the present. In either case, we in the present have to read those texts in order to understand them at all; but in seeking to understand them we—like all Muslims throughout history—bring to our reading of those past texts the frameworks of understanding of our own time and place. We hear the past voices that speak to us speaking with contemporary accents, as it were—our own. So we are always, like all the great *ulama* of the past—even if they were not aware of it—both reading the present back into the past from which we seek contemporary guidance, and also left with the problem—even if and where we think we know clearly and authoritatively what the past is telling us—of deciding *how* we are now to implement or proceed upon that understanding.

Here, too, in making decisions of this kind—even concerning implementation in our own times and circumstances of the eternal imperatives of the *Qur'an*—we bring to that process of interpretation and decision our own contemporary understandings. We cannot do otherwise. Both the eternal text of the *Qur'an* and the historical, contingent texts of the *sunna* and *shari'a* are read and humanly understood by living people—*ulama* and other believers—of their own particular time and place. Our history, our past never speaks to us directly, and even the *Qur'an*—however it speaks to us—is only heard and understood by real living people, limited in the ways and by the circumstances of their own time.

All our understanding is imperfect, human, historical and provisional—and capable, accordingly, of being changed and even deepened in the light of changing circumstances of a constantly unfolding future in ways that, in the very nature of the case, it is impossible for us now to anticipate or even imagine. The past, in whose light we wish to read and find guidance for the present, is itself known only through an image into whose formation our own present enters. In Islam there are things that are divine and eternal, but they are only ever known by humans in forms that are stamped, and also limited, by the historicity of all human understanding.

Islam's historical inception was in the divine message that the Prophet Muhammad received and transmitted. The situation in which Islam came into historical existence involved both the reception of that prophecy and the actualisation of that prophetic message by the Prophet Muhammad in Mecca and then Medina. The short period following his death, (C.E. 632-661)—that is, prior to the ascendancy of Ummayyad rule (C.E. 661-750)—established the administrative pattern which is accepted as a model by Sunni Muslims but which remained contentious for the Shi'a, who recognised a legitimate model of governance only in the rule of Ali.

> The Prophet's death temporarily paralysed his followers; even his closest Companions were not prepared for that eventuality and, having lost their mentor, did not know how to handle the new faith as well as the new state he had bequeathed them. Every group, and within every group its respective leaders, had their own views on every administrative aspect. It was not so much the religious but the political implications that bothered them (Rafiq Zakaria 1988: 43).

Whilst obeying the injunctions of the *Qur'an* and respecting the traditions laid down by the Prophet, in the period immediately following his death each of the four rightly-guided companion-caliphs had to innovate a great deal in order to meet the changing demands and differing backgrounds of their subjects. In the process the shape of what emerged as the Islamic "state" inevitably altered.

This cardinally important historical fact means little, however, to most of today's Islamic activists who seek the reactualising under modern conditions, according to their own static and historically idealised models, of an "Islamic state". The historicity of both the first model of Medinan society and the rather different early models of state and society that emerged under the first four rightly-guided caliphs hardly seem to matter to many of these activists or to affect the sociopolitical models that they offer to modern people from the Islamic past. They find in early Islamic history a model for contemporary reality, but what they find and value in it are its contingent particularities—historical but not understood historically by them—not its universal principles and aspirations.

Worldview, history and the legitimation of political agendas

Sacred worldviews, as Clifford Geertz (1973) has suggested, provide us with models of reality in two distinct and important senses; but what is most important about them is the way in which these two different but complexly interrelated senses—or the kind of models which they provide—underpin and reinforce each other. They provide us with both models *of* and models *for* reality: descriptive models of how the world really is and ethical or normative models of how we ought to behave. The former we believe we draw into ourselves from our experience, through our senses; they are the world acting upon and informing us about its inner nature, about how reality "really" is. The latter are models of action, paradigms for behaviour, that we enact within and upon the world.

Because they are so closely interrelated, Geertz suggests, they convince us that the world as we experience it is consistent with our ideas concerning how we should behave ethically in it. Our moral system is made to appear to us as arising from and consistent with nature itself, and is therefore made to appear "natural", not arbitrary; while we are at the same time also reassured, by the reverse mechanism, that nature itself is not random or arbitrary or morally indifferent, but is structured in a way that conforms with our own moral expectations of the universe and makes them reasonable. The world as it is becomes congruent with our ideas of how it should be; and our ideas of how things really should be are saved from arbitrariness and made seemingly to grow out of and reflect the way the world actually is.

It is the hidden circularity in this mechanism that lends coherence to our cultures—between their cognitive, aesthetic and moral dimensions—and between the cultures that we inhabit and our experience of the world. Through this circular reflex, cultures persuade us of their coherence and human adequacy, and thereby legitimate themselves.

Geertz's approach has been adopted by a leading contemporary analyst of Islamic society, Bassam Tibi, to explore Islam's contemporary accommodation of rapid social change, and within that context to probe the thinking of the activists of the Islamic resurgence who seek to reinstitute a supposedly "classical" Islamic state or polity. Geertz's approach provides Bassam Tibi with a way of showing how change is accommodated by being denied; of how the idea of history is used by Islamic activists to deny history and to subvert historical understanding of Islam's own development and present situation.

Using Geertz's ideas about the two mutually reinforcing kinds of models that are to be found in the sacred worldviews at the heart of all cultures, Bassam Tibi (1991) analyses the same circularity in the Islamic resurgents' worldview and ideas of history that were analysed above. The resurgents urge as mandatory the reinstitution of an Islamic state and argue that the implementation of such a state would be feasible and consistent with modern reality. But their very ideas of the past are shaped by the present and by their own present political objectives, which they read back into the past. It is therefore always the present, and their own contemporary political agendas, which are speaking to them when they believe they hear a mandatory Islamic past commanding them.

Those who most invoke history as their guide are the least historically-minded, for they fail to recognise that the past which they revere is a mirage. It is simply an image into which, unknown to themselves, they read their own times and ideas. But this very circularity, as in the case of Geertz's analysis of worldviews, is persuasive. Because it is hidden, it persuades them that the ideas which they would like to have about the world and about history are views that they are in fact entitled to have, and which history requires them to uphold. Their model of the Islamic past is a model for the Islamic present and future; but that model of the Islamic past is not grounded in any objective past but is provided by the view and direction into the future that their own political agenda sets. The model *of* the Islamic political past and the model *for* the Islamic political present and future reinforce and validate one another—because they are basically the same thing. This circularity enables the resurgents to persuade themselves that what they simply desire is nothing other than what they are divinely obliged to do.

It is no wonder, then, that so much of the resurgents' ideology is fundamentally circular, oscillating back and forth between two parts of a duality that are mirror images of each other. The fundamentalists' perspective upon change is mainly based on their understanding of Islamic doctrine which combines two conflicting concepts of development: a forward-looking option for the future and humanity, toward which one is supposed to work and within which humanity will become united under the banner of Islam; and a backward-looking interpretation of history that is bound up with the aspiration of restoring the original Islamic community of Medina.(2)

The need to address this basic question of "historicity" was acknowledged by Fazlur Rahman (1982), but he was unable to propose an answer that was as perceptive as his recognition of the problem. His explanation of the problem was that although they have a strong belief in the efficacy of the revelation in providing true answers to virtually all situations, Muslims have not squarely addressed the basic questions of method and hermeneutics that are necessary for theorising any successful yet religiously authentic engagement with modernity. This is a discerning observation, a useful diagnosis.

But the solution that he offered was simply that Muslims should seek a new methodology of Quran'ic interpretation. This prescription is disappointingly thin. The issue, the required remedy, is not simply to propose the offering of new kinds or grounds of doctrinal interpretation but to identify and remove the accumulated social, cultural and historical impediments that had long obstructed genuinely and adventurously progressive thinking within Muslim intellectual culture. The problem, that is, is not simply to think brave new thoughts, to offer liberating new interpretations, as a purely intellectual or textual exercise, but rather—as the necessary prerequisite for such thinking—to engage in a searching critique and reform of Muslim intellectual practice itself as a political and social phenomenon. So long as that social practice and its sociopolitical and cultural contexts remain unaltered, unchallenged, and not even adequately criticised or understood, no new kinds of thinking that would be adequate to the task of renewal can possibly emerge.

> For Fazlur Rahman essentially the
>
> substantive or constitutive ... teaching of the Prophet and the *Qur'an* is undoubtedly for *action in this world,* since it provides guidance for man concerning his behaviour on earth in relation to other men. God exists in the mind of the believer to regulate his behaviour on earth if he is religiomorally experienced, but that which is to be regulated is the essence of the matter. The bane of later medieval Islam ... was that what was regulative, namely God, was made the exclusive object of experience and thus, instead of men's seeking values for this experience, the experience became the end in itself (1982: 14).

From the very outset, and certainly in the age of the flourishing of classical Islamic thinking, Muslims failed to recognise the problematic relationship between the act of interpreting the founding sacred text in an effort to comprehend its models for reality and the act of applying the *sunna* as model of reality. The failure to pursue this problem at great length may possibly be due to the power of the belief that there is only one truth, valid for all time and entirely unconditioned by history. But such a view both fails to recognise the difference, and also endorses the refusal to distinguish, between a single, eternal spiritual truth and the variable and historically contingent civilisational manifestations in which humans, always very partially and imperfectly, have sought to give form and expression to that transcendent truth.

Islamisation in Malaysia: Paradoxical outcomes and effects

This comprehensive failure to grasp the historicity of past Muslim political experience and intellectual practice is evident throughout, and pervasively vitiates, the project of Islamisation as it is conducted in contemporary Malaysia. Although one of the smaller Muslim countries in Asia, Malaysia is one of the most developed economically among the developing Muslim nations. For this reason, it provides a sharp illustration of the dilemma faced by contemporary Muslim societies all over the world, as they pursue transformative economic growth yet seek to maintain intact their cultural integrity and religious authenticity. Impelled by the rapid industrialisation of its economy over the past seven to ten years, Malaysia has sought to combine ever more comprehensive and accelerated Islamisation policies with a growing modernity of lifestyle and material culture.

The contradictions posed by these two sets of policies underline the nature and complexity of the political and cultural context in which the Malaysian Islamising ideology, in both its government and oppositional manifestations, operates. Indeed, in significant part, the state's current Islamisation projects have been undertaken under some considerable political pressure, especially the constraints imposed by the government's need to legitimate itself as Islamic against the claims of traditionalising or alternative neo-traditionalist Islamic political forces: notably, the Islamic Party PAS, the Muslim youth movement ABIM and the *Darul Arqam* movement which combines communitarian economic entrepreneurialism with the pursuit of what its adherents consider as a lifestyle of pristine Medinan simplicity based on the Prophet's *sunna*. As a result of its rivalry with these activist Islamic alternatives—and its desire not to seem less committed than they to the cause of Islam—the present government is constantly driven to adopt policies and strategies that contradict its own agenda not of consolidating Muslim neo-traditionalism but of encouraging a Muslim culture of modernity.

Malaysian Muslims do not yet possess the intellectual integrity and cultural strength to define their own project of Islamic modernity in opposition, or at least contradistinction, both to various dominant Westernising forces that they reject and to the traditionalising, repressive, and often coercive Islamism that is imported from the Middle East by a variety of Islamic movements and organisations. But while denunciation of Western influence generally and animosity towards Islam in particular are common, and even encouraged on all sides, very few Malaysians dare or even seem inclined to oppose the claims of Islamic moral and political authoritarianism. Whether their silence is motivated more by indifference or apathy than fear or prudence remains arguable. Meanwhile, the government seemingly still wishes to pursue the project of fashioning an Islamic culture of modernity but, as was suggested, it is always inhibited from doing so effectively by its own prudent desire not to seem "un-Islamic" or even "secular" in comparison with its activist Islamic political rivals.

As a result, many of the Islamisation policies hitherto promoted by the state have proved to be extremely retrogressive, especially in their effects upon women, family life, the working classes (both urban and rural), and the poor. New statutes and regulations imposed under the banner of Islamisation have merely given religious legitimacy to the reproduction of archaic and patriarchal forms of the subordination and control of women. These policies bear down heavily upon the standards of morality of these relatively poor and powerless sectors of society among the ordinary *rakyat*, but only impinge far more lightly upon the aristocracy and *nouveaux riches* who are apparently allowed to have standards of morality (or decadence, depending upon whose perspective one adopts in viewing it) of their own.

Some of the programmes that have been implemented over recent years have created contentious outcomes. For example, there is a heightened effort to spell out official Islam's "moral constructions" of the ideal Muslim woman and wife within various Islamisation discourses on gender, family and marriage. These are prominently and powerfully promoted via extensive religious programming on radio and television, in official initiatives promoting wholesome family life, and through government-sponsored Islamic family life institutes and the like. Organisations such as *Akademi Keluarga Bahagia Malaysia* (an organisation devoted to the encouragement of wholesome Muslim family life) are not only government-supported in their own activities; with government endorsement their general approach is adopted within the government itself, for example within the policies of the Ministry of Social Welfare, where they ultimately affect the personal and domestic lives of the nation's non-Muslim as well as Muslim citizens. The effects of a moralising, authoritarian and repressive Islamisation, and especially of its often sociologically simplistic understanding of social and personal problems, becomes ever more pervasive through the entire society. Non-Muslim citizens ultimately enjoy no exemption from the impact of the regressive kind of thinking that is characteristic of an intellectually narrow Islamisation.

Related to these there has also been a tendency towards the greater bureaucratisation and control of institutions of marriage and divorce. Various procedures have been put into place which govern the matrimonial intentions and conduct of Muslim citizens, putting them under more bureaucratic assessment and scrutiny. Notable examples here are the *kursus keluarga bahagia* (marriage-preparation courses) for young couples who apply to be married in Selangor or Wilayah Persekutuan (Federal Territory), and the further requirement of a special interview of prospective brides that are intended to ascertain their religious knowledge. Indirectly this bears upon the question of their "moral worth or capacity" to become wives and mothers—and also arguably abridges the religious right of Muslims (as well as their obligation) to marry.

At the same time reports are becoming more frequent of *shari'a* court decisions pertaining to new Muslim converts which allow or indirectly condone the neglect of duty and responsibility on their part for maintenance and care of their non-Muslim wives and children who have not followed them in their conversion to Islam. A number of recent cases of this kind have been or are being appealed to the nation's higher courts, prominently highlighting this problem.

Islamisation initiatives in Malaysia have also given licence to the surveillance not only of the actions but even the thinking of the country's Muslim citizens. As in quite different political and historical contexts, moral zeal and an eagerness to reform the world in accordance with a splendid vision have encouraged efforts to impose a monolithic, uniformitarian social ethic. (Soviet Russia and Communist China with their state ideologies for the family and their "socialisation programme" to cultivate good workers and citizens of the state come to mind here.)

One notable example of this tendency has been a recent announcement that a network of religious rehabilitation centres—modelled upon the nation's draconian drug rehabilitation camps with their quasi-military regimen—is to be established for those with unacceptable religious views. One of the key criteria that have been announced of such unacceptability is a tendency to oppose, criticise, or show disrespect for the *ulama*, their religious leadership and opinions. Such measures are urged and endorsed by the state-supporting and state-supported *ulama* themselves, despite the dubious propriety of these measures in Islamic principle. The readiness of the leading *ulama* who hold official government positions to have recourse to such measures for further entrenching their own position is suggestive of the emergence of a form of clericalism that runs altogether counter to basic Muslim doctrine. That the right of opening the gates of thinking (*ijtihad*) should be claimed and treated as the monopoly of so defensive and closed-minded a group of Muslims must disturb the authentically traditional Muslim conscience as much as it does the modernist's.

The disquieting cumulative effect of this bundle of Islamisation legislation has been to reinforce a number of authoritarian, feudal and actually quite un-Islamic political practices, most notably the use of force to ensure that citizens submit unquestioningly to authority. Such coerced submission may have many precedents in the less than ideal course of Islamic political and dynastic history, but it has no warrant in Islamic religious and social ideals. Yet the arguments and discourse of this authoritarian Islamisation have promoted only the narrowest of politics based upon self-righteous ideologies. They have encouraged a regrettable narrow-mindedness in religious socialisation and outlook that has resulted in what can only be called "religious illiteracy", a form of "closing of the Muslim mind".

Contrary to the urgings of individual moral autonomy and responsibility that characterise Qur'anic Islam, Malaysian Muslims are routinely cautioned not to question the knowledge and authority of the various *imam, ulama* and Islamic court judges. At the same time, there is a palpable government preoccupation with maintaining surveillance of all non-state-sponsored Islamic movements such as the *Darul Arqam* and *Tabligh* movements, small coteries of modernist Muslims who debate the undoubted historicity and question the purportedly sacred and mandatory character of *hadith* as a source of law, and Shi'a Muslims, who are frequently spoken of in official government releases as if Shi'a were not historically and doctrinally an integral component of Islam.

At the same time the emphasis placed by the fundamentalists upon externals and upon the mere signs of zealous conformity has led among some of the activist Islamisation groups to a new "kind of *shirik*" (compromising the principle of divine unity and singularity by attributing to others qualities that are God's alone). Some of the activists make a fetish of the outward signs of piety that they affect for themselves and urge upon others, to the point where these externals become political and also religious "icons", as it were.

Indeed, the kind of "cult of personality" that has grown up around some of the major figures of the Islamic resurgence and the kind of hero-worship that is directed towards them ought to be a cause of justifiable concern to Muslims of principled and discerning religious fastidiousness. For example, the ideas of such figures as Maududi, Syed Qutb, and Hasan al-Banna are now increasingly treated with great reverence and upheld with enormous zeal; so much so that Muslims of good faith but different inclination cannot even attempt to criticise their thought without incurring strong indignation from the new generation of their supporters. Criticism of merely the ideas or approach of such thinkers and noted *ulama* is treated as an assault upon Islam itself, as a form of treachery or apostasy. Rather than responding to honest criticism with a call for open debate of the ideas and issues in question, earnest supporters of the hero figures of activist Islamisation treat any questioning of their leaders' ideas as tantamount to sacrilege. But idolising these individuals comes close to making "idols" of them, with all that it entails for the foundations of Muslim faith.

Recent cases in Egypt (where modernist writers have been murdered and scholars been declared apostates) and elsewhere provide further evidence of how such misdirected zeal may encourage intolerance. This violence, actual and threatened, amounts to religiously unacceptable intimidation, directed against fellow individual Muslims who have merely dared to express doubts and offer strong criticism of current Islamisation initiatives. The same outlook and inclination, even if it has not led to the same extreme actions, has not been entirely unknown in Malaysia, where any such manifestation must be counted as disturbing.

One can only hope that such examples of the radical militancy of some activist Islamising groups will not be imported here. However, what is happening in religious life mirrors what is happening more broadly in Malaysian society under the impact of accelerated modernisation. The restrictive effects of official Islamisation strategies upon individual autonomy in thought and action are reinforced by parallel constraints in the working, associational, and public life of Malaysians. The dissuasion exerted against notions of active participatory citizenship is sometimes obvious, but often it is conveyed quite subtly. The accompanying justification of such constraint on such grounds as "national security" and the need "not to jeopardise our economic prosperity and growth" or "to undermine our political stability" unnecessarily inhibits legitimate dissent and the expression of critical public opinion. As the country's push towards industrialisation gains momentum, Malaysian Muslims—in common with all Malaysians—are experiencing a tightening of controls on citizen participation in all spheres of public and political life, not just the religious. But they are also experiencing additional constraint as Muslims, because of the increasing pressures from the growing assertiveness of a backward-looking and authoritarian religious conformism.

Conclusion

The overall effect of recent developments has been to strengthen the position of the state as both sponsor and beneficiary of a variety of Islamisation initiatives. While, at times ambivalently, the government has supported these Islamisation measures, often in the effort to advance or buttress its legitimacy in the face of Islamic activist criticism and opposition, this strategy has often rebounded. Ironically, state-sponsored and state-funded Islamisation programmes have often fallen into the hands of the government's opponents and been used against it—or at least to generate resistance to the state's own modernisation agenda.

Under the combined effect of these economic and religious policies, Malaysia can seemingly hope to produce nothing but new generations of Muslims with closed minds who, as the highest expression of their faith, aspire only to an intensified ritualising of formal, supposedly "orthodox" practice. What stands to be lost or neglected, at both the individual and public levels, as a result of this advancing religious formalism and sociopolitical inhibition is the inner spiritual, moral, and intellectual growth of the Malaysian Muslim community. Malaysia in consequence may well forfeit the historic opportunity with which its favourable economic prospects might provide it: the opportunity to play a pioneering role for change within the worldwide *umma* in the creation of an authentically Muslim culture of modernity.

The nation's Vision 2020 agenda urges Malaysia's development, not simply as a fully modernised economy, but as a fully modernised society, grounded in a recognisably Malay "culture of modernity". A central component of modern

Malaysian culture in this vision is a modernised Malay culture, and this in turn implies a modernised Malay culture that is animated by an authentically Muslim culture of modernity. Yet such a Muslim modernity is something that all the state apparatus of modernist Islamisation (including its specialist research institutes) has altogether failed to produce.

However, as a number of leading contemporary Muslim thinkers (such as the Maghribi historian Hichem Djaït) have argued, Muslim societies must resist wholesale "Westernisation" and "dis-*orient*-ation" (the pun here of losing one's "easternness" to Western domination is intentional). That is, Muslims must resist surrendering cultural authenticity, in the name of modernisation and modernity, as the fundamentalist activists also argue. But they must not do so by following the fundamentalist agenda. Rather, the challenge is not simply to cultivate Islamic religious modernism once more—to resume yet again Muhammad Abduh's project of religious renewal one hundred years after his time. The task instead is to modernise Muslim culture, to create an authentic Muslim culture of modernity—and in that way, to provide today's Muslims with their own religiously and culturally authentic ways of participating in modernity. Modern Muslims need to become capable of engaging with, yet at the same time also resisting, the West's own culture of modernity: by devising for themselves authentically Islamic ways in which they may both contribute to and participate within an emerging universal, worldwide culture of modernity. This, and not a regressive and authoritarian Islamisation that flees from history, is what modern Muslims—and nations with Muslim majorities such as Malaysia—need to pursue.

Endnotes

1. The analysis offered in this paper is a phenomenological one inspired by a reading of Bassam Tibi's book *The Crisis of Modern Islam: A Preindustrial Culture in the Scientific-Technological Age* (1988). Since then the same author has expanded his "cultural thesis" in a subsequent work entitled *Islam and the Cultural Accommodation of Social Change* (1990; available in a paperback edition since October 1991).

Bassam Tibi, a Syrian-born scholar now based in Germany after leaving Egypt, is essentially concerned with the cultural, political and economic malaise in the Middle East. He argues in the earlier book (1988) that through a historical study of the development and decline of Islamic civilisation one discovers that the incorporation of external ideas into a culture is not only a common phenomenon but one that can be proven to be beneficial rather than detrimental. He points out that early Islamic culture absorbed a rich measure of Greek thought (the so-called Hellenisation of Islamic philosophy), adopted aspects of Indian medicine, and appropriated principles of administration—all without any uneasiness over the assumption of non-Arab or non-Islamic cultural elements. Tibi wonders whether this phenomenon may again be repeated; that is, can modern technological-scientific culture also be incorporated into Islam without friction? Tibi defines his work within the discipline of sociology of religion; his objective is to view religion as a cultural phenomenon—as a dimension of culture, as political ideology, and as entailing rituals of repoliticisation. His intention is not to show how every social phenomenon or problem can be explained or solved by the interpretation of Islamic texts, but rather to scrutinise the intellectual and cultural bases of social behaviour and praxis of Muslim societies.

In his more recent research, Tibi revises his earlier approach by undertaking an analysis of Islam mainly as a cultural system in its own right. He seeks to understand Islam as a system of cultural symbols through which Muslims perceive reality and evolve their worldview. His discussion considers whether "culture" is a phenomenon that shapes a society, and how Islamic values and the politicisation of the sacred in the Islamic Middle East are used as an instrument for the legitimation of power.

Developing his framework from Clifford Geertz's interpretative study of religion "as a cultural system", Tibi attempts to go beyond Geertz by also locating the cultural phenomenon of contemporary Islam within the context of international relations. It is in this context that his discussion gives particular attention to, and places a special importance upon, the evolution of Islamic educational institutions.

Tibi is concerned with the role of these educational institutions, including both those of mass education and those of higher education and research: as national articulators of change under the aegis of Islamisation projects and as critics of the West and Eurocentrism. That is, the institutions of Muslim education and Islamic cultural reproduction have not escaped the pressures of regressive or historically nostalgic rather than forward-looking Islamisation; they have therefore often impeded rather than assisted the efforts of Muslim nations to find some adequate intellectual basis for responding effectively to and countering Western modernity.

This fact remains ironically and even tragically true, according to Tibi, of those very institutions of higher education that have been created with the specific mission of empowering Islam intellectually and culturally to address Western modernity and to redress Islam's historic subordination to it. This point has some bearing upon the failure of a variety of such new, government-sponsored Islamic educational and research institutions in Malaysia really to meet, or even understand, the challenge that faces them.

2. For example, see Muhammad Mumtaz Ali's study of *The Islamic Concepts of Ummah and Shari'a*, Petaling Jaya: Pelanduk Publications, 1992, which calls for the establishment of a world *umma* under a restored caliphate.

References

Abdullahi Ahmed An-Na'im, *Toward an Islamic Reformation: Civil Liberties, Human Rights, and International Law.* Syracuse, NY: Syracuse University Press, 1990.

Bassam Tibi, *The Crisis of Modern Islam: A Preindustrial, Culture in the Scientific-Technological Age,* trans. J. von Sivers. Salt Lake City: University of Utah Press, 1988.

————, *Islam and the Cultural Accommodation of Social Change,* trans. C. Krojzl. Boulder: Westview Press, 1990.

Fazlur Rahman, *Islam and Modernity.* Chicago: The University of Chicago Press, 1982.

Fuad I. Khuri, *Imams and Emirs: State, Religion and Sects in Islam.* London: Saqi Books, 1990.

Geertz, C., "Religion as a Cultural System" in *The Interpretation of Cultures: Selected Essays.* New York: Basic Books, 1973.

Hichem Djaït, *Europe and Islam: Cultures and Modernity,* trans. P. Heinegg. Berkeley: University of California Press, 1985.

Mayer, A. E., *Islam and Human Rights: Tradition and Politics.* Boulder, Co.: Westview Press, 1991.

Muhammad Mumtaz Ali, *The Islamic Concepts of Ummah and Shari'a.* Petaling Jaya: Pelanduk Publications, 1992.

Rafiq Zakaria, *The Struggle Within Islam: The Conflict Between Religion and Politics.* Harmondsworth: Penguin Books, 1988.

Epilogue:

Shari'a Law in the Modern World

14

Hudud Law or Islamic Modernity?

*Norani Othman**

Supported by all 36 members of the State Assembly including two from the Barisan Nasional, the Kelantan Syariah Criminal Code (II) Bill 1993 was unanimously adopted by the Kelantan State Assembly on 25 November 1993.

This bill seeks to give effect to a certain understanding of *shari'a* criminal law including the *hudud, qisas* and *ta'azir* offences and their punishments.

Not surprisingly, the most contentious aspect of the bill is its provisions for enforcing the so-called *hudud* punishments. These

* *Sisters In Islam* have sought to articulate a principled Islamic modernist response to proposals for the enforcement of the *hudud* punishments since 1990, when the enactment of those punishments in Kelantan began to be mooted. They have written newspaper and magazine articles, attended forums held by proponents of *hudud* enforcement, organised seminars and forums of their own, and in January 1994 they submitted a memorandum on the subject to Prime Minister Datuk Seri Dr. Mahathir Mohamad. On all these occasions, they argued that there is more to Islam than *shari'a,* more to *shari'a* than *hudud,* and that Islam, *shari'a* and *hudud* all have to be understood historically. At the time of preparation of that memorandum, and while this book was in the final stages of production, Norani Othman wrote this commentary amplifying the grounds of the *Sisters In Islam* memorandum; it appeared in a slightly different form as the "Saturday Forum" column in the *New Straits Times* on 29 January 1994.

require that those found guilty of certain offences (such as adultery, armed robbery and apostasy, for example) should be subjected in public to punishments including flogging, mutilation of limbs by amputation, stoning to death, and crucifixion.

Two views of Islamic law

The drive to enforce *shari'a* law including, most prominently, the imposition of these *hudud* punishments is not confined to Kelantan or Malaysia but is found, though rarely as a majority tendency, throughout the contemporary Muslim world.

The attempt to reintroduce what Islam's early generations understood as Islamic law has been characteristic of one response to the modern Muslim predicament.

After the glories of its early history, Islam was in early modern times eclipsed by the West. Many Muslims wondered how this humiliating and demoralising setback was to be addressed.

For some, the way forward was to do what the West itself had done, but better and in one's own way: that is, to embrace modernity, but to find an authentically Muslim way of doing so, consistent with the progressive, rational, morally egalitarian, emancipatory, and democratic spirit of the *Qur'an* itself.

But for others, a different path seemed indicated. If Islam had been eclipsed, then the way to its restoration was by a return to the sociopolitical institutions, laws and practices of the triumphant early *umma*, especially those of the first generation of Muslims who lived under the Prophet Muhammad's leadership in Medina.

The first tendency is that of Islamic modernism, both religious and social. It is the tradition which, in common with their predecessors, Malaysia's current political leaders notably exemplify. This is an approach which sees every generation as not merely entitled but also obliged to rethink Islam anew, in an effort to find new and ever more inclusive ways of giving effect to its enduring social and moral imperatives.

For this approach, history as it unfolds holds out new and ever greater possibilities for the actualisation of the Qur'anic ethical and social vision—and of giving constantly evolving sociolegal form to those new possibilities and understandings—that were not available to previous Muslim generations, including even the wisest thinkers and noblest spirits among them.

To the adherents of the second approach, who seek to move Islam forward by taking the *umma* back to the supposed security of its past practices, the early generations of Islam—being closer to the life and example of the Prophet himself—were giants, or at least exemplars, who necessarily knew better from their involvement in early Islamic history than do we, or any of their successors ever could.

For the supporters of this second approach, as for all Muslims, the *Qur'an* itself is divine, sacred and authoritative. But they also treat as virtually no less authoritative and binding the interpretations of that sacred text that were made—under the often limiting sociolegal conditions then prevailing—by the early Muslim legal scholars who codified Islamic law in its traditional or classical formulations.

For the adherents of this approach, history offers not new possibilities but imposes a troubling remoteness, even alienation. As history advances, it takes the *umma* ever further away from the paradigmatic ideal of its founding generations, from the secure example and guidance of those who enjoyed a direct understanding of Islam in its authentic and formative phase.

For them, accordingly, the way to close that gap—to heal the wounding distance imposed upon modern Muslims by relentlessly advancing history—is to reaffirm and to reimpose in the present the understandings of Qur'anic ethical imperatives of those early times: that is, as they were first codified in their not simply premodern but actually most archaic legal forms.

Seen in this way, the desire to implement what its proponents regard as the essence of Islamic law—including the *hudud* punishments—becomes understandable. But it can also be recognised for what it really is: an anachronistic attempt to impose in modern times and upon modern Muslims of good faith what is not the essence or culmination of Islamic law but only Islamic law in its most archaic, provisional and historically unevolved form.

Historical understanding, not apostasy

To point to the historical context and character of those early legal codifications (including the *hudud* provisions) of the Qur'anic imperatives is simply to understand the evolution of the Muslim faith and Islamic law historically. It is not to commit apostasy.

Throughout Islamic history many Muslims have questioned and debated how best this law might be codified and applied. Indeed, that is precisely the process through which classical Islamic law itself evolved.

The actualisation of *shari'a* principles as codified law, including the *hudud*, emerged in such debates from the opinions (*fiqh*) of jurists and scholars. Formed through a methodology of interpretation (*ijtihad, qiyas*), their views were given subsequent sanction through the political process (*ijma*, or the consensus of the jurists of a particular time and place). But consensus is not necessarily unanimity; it was often only majority opinion, and was at best only human inference, not a divine injunction.

These scholars based their reasoning upon a divine source of law. In addition, the process of reasoning through which, by interpreting the sacred sources, they fashioned the law was also for them a religiously sanctioned one. But their activities and the legal culture that they produced were human achievements, not divinely bestowed.

As such, their efforts were historical, provisional and imperfect. They accordingly can and must be treated both historically and critically. The question of apostasy simply cannot arise here (though to treat the products of human endeavour as divine, as some of the proponents of the Kelantan bill do when insisting that implementation of the *hudud* is mandatory because divinely enjoined, comes very close to *shirik*, or compromising the principle of God's unity).

Yet even before its enactment by the Kelantan State Legislative Assembly, the proponents of the recent bill passed explicit judgements of apostasy on those who might question or oppose it (for example, in their public forum on 17 October 1993 in Kuala Lumpur; see the *New Straits Times*, 19 October 1993).

Dilemmas of implementation

The questionable impact of implementing Muslim criminal law has been documented in a number of Muslim countries. The experience of countries such as Iran, the Sudan and Pakistan has demonstrated how problematic—and even *zalim* or cruel—the effects can be of seeking to implement Islamic law (or rather, certain historically limited understandings of its principles and intentions).

That experience highlights the need, prior to any such attempted implementation, for careful and intellectually searching attention to be given to the bases of the interpretation of *shari'a* law; to the manner and the different cultural context of its past evolution; and to the undesirable consequences of any anachronistic application of *shari'a* principles to modern conditions in historically archaic forms or via premodern codifications.

The Kelantan bill accordingly requires our careful scrutiny. It is the religious duty of the *umma* to ensure that the recent Kelantan enactment does not contravene, in either its letter or spirit, the eternal principles of justice and equality that are not only enjoined by the *Qur'an* but which, in fact, it is the central purpose of any proposed codification of *shari'a* to uphold and protect.

Vision 2020, Islamic modernity and shari'a renewal

The debate whether countries that regard themselves as Muslim should implement the *hudud* punishments as part of their efforts to actualise a modern Islamic system of criminal justice remains a contentious one. Many in Malaysia today are anxiously awaiting the federal government's decision whether it will permit implementation of the *hudud* laws in Kelantan.

A crucial question confronts members of the *umma* as they await that decision. Must Muslim societies today implement the *hudud* and *qisas* punishments as understood by the founding Muslim scholars and jurists of the past (even though those punishments are simply conventional, time-bound formulations of Islamic criminal law that were offered by Muslim jurists in the second to third century after *hijrah*)?

Or, alternatively, are contemporary Muslim societies entitled to reformulate traditional notions of *shari'a* justice according to their own circumstances, based on modern understandings of eternal Qur'anic principles and Islamic teachings, and in so doing to revitalise *shari'a* itself?

To many in Malaysia who regard the recent Kelantan enactment with apprehension, and for similarly minded Muslim modernists throughout the *umma*, the second of these options seems the appropriate way to create a humane and practical Islamic criminal legal system consistent with the eternal Qur'anic imperatives of social and legal justice.

That approach, rather than insisting upon the anachronistic imposition of premodern forms and understandings of *shari'a* law, seems the only possible basis for creating the kind of Islamic culture of modernity that Muslim modernists of the last century and more have sought.

That aspiration has not only guided the thinking of the Islamic modernist movement as a whole. It also animates Malaysia's present leaders and the Vision 2020 agenda to which they and the nation as a whole are committed.

Our drive as a nation towards industrialisation, Prime Minister Datuk Seri Dr. Mahathir Mohamad has made clear, envisages the creation of a fully modern society based upon a Malaysian culture of modernity.

An authentically Malaysian modernity must include, and itself be grounded upon, an Islamic culture of modernity. The anachronistic enforcement of premodern understandings of Islamic law, as in the Kelantan *hudud* bill, seems hardly congruent with the creation of an Islamic culture of modernity—or, indeed, with any principled project for the modern sociolegal realisation of enduring Qur'anic imperatives.

Beyond conventional ijtihad

Those who codified Islamic law in its premodern forms were simply human beings who sought to offer the best understanding of the eternal Qur'anic message that was possible for them in their time.

We, in our time, are both entitled and required to do no less. But we can do better than the best minds of earlier Muslim generations, and so need not be limited by their understandings and achievements.

We can do better, not because we are better than our predecessors but because we are better placed to do so. All the great changes that have led to the emergence of the modern world provide this generation of Muslims with opportunities to understand and actualise Islam in ways that were not available to our predecessors.

They provide enlightened Muslims of this era with unprecedented opportunities to seek the realisation of the essential and universal message of Islam; in particular, to give expression to its sociolegal aspirations in a far more profound and just form than was ever possible under the constraints and circumstances that limited even the best and most noble thinkers of earlier Islamic civilisation.

But there remain obstacles to the realisation of this challenge. Contrary to the urgings of individual moral autonomy and responsibility (*taqwa*) that characterise Qur'anic Islam, Malaysian Muslims are routinely cautioned—as in the all too muted and constrained debate over the recent Kelantan *hudud* law enactment—not to question the knowledge and authority of the *imam* and *ulama*. Deference to them is made the sign of piety and the proof of faith.

Yet the argument offered here clearly entails that, as part of their efforts to fashion such an Islamic culture of modernity, forward-looking Muslims in Malaysia—and elsewhere in the worldwide *umma*—will have to devise and make use of new methods of sociolegal and religious reasoning.

Renewal (*islah*) and innovation (*tajdid*)—in general, an Islamic culture of modernity that is congruent with the Islamic principle of a reasoned participatory activism—will require action on a basis that goes beyond conventional understandings of *ijtihad*.

The new understanding of *ijtihad* presumed by the idea of an Islamic culture of modernity entails a dual recognition: of the moral autonomy and responsibility of the thinking Muslim individual; and of the need for the process of "ijtihadic" reasoning in which those individuals are involved to be conducted not anarchically but in a dialogical or communitarian manner within the *umma*.

This is not a proposal for "disenfranchising" the *ulama*. Rather, it is an argument that, consistent both with the spirit of modernity and the central principles of Islam in its formative moment, the *ulama* must democratise their procedures and practice.

That is, they must learn to exercise their own *ijtihad* in cooperative engagement together with the "laity" or ordinary members of the *umma*.

Their own continuing role will depend upon their learning to do so as part of a common endeavour to give expression to the enduring principles of our common faith: in ways and forms, including within forms of sociolegal reasoning and through the devising of legal institutions, that are appropriate to the dignity of modern believers and the times in which we all now live.

Index